CHRIST'S
suburban body

To Bob & Jean —

Thanks for being who you are. We miss you like everything around here, but your contribution of time & talent continues to be multiplied.

Peace

Bill

May 1970

P.S. god is still a meringue

CHRIST'S
suburban body

Wilfred M. Bailey
&
William K. McElvaney

ABINGDON PRESS
Nashville
New York

CHRIST'S SUBURBAN BODY

Copyright © 1970 by Abingdon Press

ISBN 0-687-07858-X

Library of Congress Catalog Card Number: 79-109672

SET UP, PRINTED, AND BOUND BY THE
PARTHENON   PRESS,   AT   NASHVILLE,
TENNESSEE, UNITED STATES OF AMERICA

contents

preface

The Communist Party would give its right arm for access to a "cigar box with a steeple on it" at every crossroad and village where people meet at least once a week. A guy who overlooks that setup as an operational base doesn't know what it means to be a revolutionary. . . . In four years, the whirlpools of renewal around our country in the local congregation are going to be flowing like rivulets. In twelve years the renewal will be like a mighty tide— *An Expert on the Church*[1]

Let us have no illusions: the revolutionary struggle will be fought out elsewhere, and those who fight the battle for the future of man will hardly be inclined to look to Christian faith for a relevant or redeeming word.—*Another Expert on the Church*[2]

These two statements by veteran church "insiders" are characteristic of the polarized opinions about the church in our time. Perhaps never before has there been the simultaneous optimism and pessimism about the church's present and future that can be found in churchmen today. While some persons foresee a mighty tide of revolutionary renewal

[1] Joseph W. Mathews in *Together* magazine, March, 1966, p. 49.
[2] Richard Shaull, in the seventh lecture in the Senior Colloquy, Perkins School of Theology, October, 1967. The statement indicates the future for the church seen by Professor Shaull unless we are willing to pay the price of a Christian presence in a revolutionary world. He believes the possibility is slight for such a presence.

within the church, others have already written off the church in any conceivable form. The finest hour for the church is beginning to dawn, according to the apostles of hope. Others are convinced that time spent in resuscitating the church in a secular age is an exercise in futility.

At least equally significant is that these contrasting viewpoints are frequently found side by side *within the same person.* On occasions we experience the church truly caring for the world, risking its neck and pioneering into the outer space of human needs and relationships. In those moments we say to ourselves, "The church is free to be the church. This is life at its best." To those who love the church there is no headier wine than the community of faith fulfilling its reason for being—steward of the humane vision, servant of justice, shepherd of the wounded, reconciler of the divided. On other occasions we can barely escape the conclusion that the church has begun to awaken too late, that somehow the roaring revolutions of mankind have left the church behind as a quaint reminder of a past age. And so an internal tug-of-war constantly pulls us back and forth toward opposite poles of opinion.

Many factors contribute to the shifting convictions concerning the relevance of today's church. The sheer complexity of a rapidly changing urban culture tends to produce question marks about all functions and roles—the church, the family, the arts, private enterprise, education, government, and the whole cultural milieu. In a time of rapid change we are forced to review constantly the why, the what, and the how of our individual and institutional lives. Almost every community in which we participate is forever analyzing once again "the nature of the group." In the case of the authors, our wives have playfully teased us about being devotees of "nature study." We are ceaselessly reformulating in one group or another the nature of the church, the nature of a commission or task group, the nature of preaching, and so on. "Nature study" is a sign of the changing times in which we live out the gift of our lives.

One's evaluation of the relevance of the church may also depend in part on one's interpretation of what that relevance *should be.* For example, suppose that one person expects the church to be a revolutionary agent of social change. Suppose further that another person expects the church to be no more than a nourisher and sustainer of persons through worship, instruction, and various forms of shepherding. Obviously for these two persons the evaluations of the church's ministry and its effectiveness are operating on dissimilar premises in the beginning.

In other words, according to one evaluator's premise, a congregation could be judged as extremely relevant due to its liturgical vitality, its creative ministry to residential families, and its care of the sick and the aged. But by the definition of mission as responsible involvement in public life, the same congregation could be seen as essentially irrelevant.

Relevance in the eyes of many churchmen has to do not only with definition of mission, but also with rate of progress toward the defined mission. A churchman who demands a revolutionary rate of change in the church may become utterly disgusted and leave the institutional church. But a colleague with the same ultimate goals for the church who accepts an evolutionary pace may be so sufficiently satisfied with the integrity and progress of the church that he will continue his work in it. The "evolutionary" sometimes works out of the conviction that, human nature being what it is, there are no other structures available which are without considerable vested interests, political in-fighting, and a certain amount of bureaucracy.

This book is about the possibilities of the suburban church as we have seen them and experienced them ourselves, and as we have observed them in Christ's suburban body throughout the nation. Our intention is to transmit signals of hope and challenge, based on the following claims: (1) The affluence and influence of the suburban scene will partly determine whether the future of America will move toward a dehumanizing or a rehumanizing style of life. (2) The suburban church could become an increasingly important factor in liberating suburban man and in helping to shape the direction and utilization of suburban power. (3) This suburban possibility of the church depends on its willingness to assume some of the characteristics of the underground church in order that new priorities and new forms can be initiated. Our intention is to speak to the non-Methodist reader, both clergyman and layman, as well as to our own heritage.

In Part I we attempt to provide images of how a suburban congregation might conceive its overall task as a community of faith. Chapter 1 suggests the urgency of the suburban ministry and the factors which have given birth to this urgency. Chapter 2 offers a theological motif, while chapter 3 points toward a functional framework through which this theological grounding can be expressed.

Part II is concerned with the practical implementation of Part I. In particular, it emphasizes one dimension of the church's mission: the intentional relationship of the church with the wider community. The fact that we have narrowed our central thrust to the church's social engagement is in no sense a depreciation of the other missional functions of the church, as will be made clear. Nor does the process of selectivity represent "a favorite interest" on the part of the authors. *The choice of emphasis allows us to concentrate our efforts in a specialized field about which, in our judgment, less material of a realistic and constructive quality has been written.*

Chapter 4 is concerned with forms of implementation. The mechanics and the work of task groups are dealt with in chapter 5. Chapter 6 is also a "how to" chapter, concerned primarily with corporate and individual action. Chapter 7 discusses ecumenics in the suburban setting, and chapter 8 focuses on questions of crisis within the church. An illustration of content for the church's missional agenda is the subject of the Appendix. Both authors affirm the content of the entire book, although the division of primary responsibility is as follows: McElvaney—Preface, Chapters 1-4, 7, and Appendix; Bailey —Chapters 5, 6, and 8.

In holding forth these signals of hope and challenge, we have attempted to combine some profiles of the suburban church throughout the United States with our own experiences in the suburban ministry. Our intention is to offer neither an exhaustive survey of everything significant now happening in the suburban church throughout the nation nor a scintillating personal success story. Any author who thinks he is doing either of these is probably fooling himself. A comprehensive survey would be out of date by the time it was researched and published because changes are occurring so rapidly. The sharing of personal experiences or of specifics in the work of a particular congregation can certainly have value for readers, especially if the failures and disappointments are also honestly reported. Otherwise, only a half-truth is offered to the reader. From time to time in our underground-aboveground journey, we will recommend other readings which seem pertinent to a particular topic.

A brief word is in order here concerning our use of the term "suburb." We use it in its simplest definition—a community lying within commuting distance of a central city. We have made no attempt to distinguish different types of suburbs, preferring instead to leave this task to the reader's own situation and knowledge. We are aware, however, that there are many kinds of suburbs—working-class and middle-class, traditional and transient, as well as differences in income levels, home-to-work traveling patterns, and age levels.

One of the factors which make the suburban ministry an intriguing proposition is the incredible potential within the suburban community. We should be haunted and hounded by questions about its future. Who will shape its potential? What decision makers will direct the value system of the mushrooming suburbs? Who will provide a prophetic word to the community on issues of common significance? What group will assume responsibility for equal opportunities, fair housing, and a creative educational system? Where will the seeds for sane models of creative dissent be sown? Who will offer a community of care and assurance? Who will remind men of their responsibilities to the total metropolitan community? Who will be hard where men are soft and soft where they are hard? These are tasks which call for the presence of a militant shepherd.

However, there is, in our case, a more personal reason why the suburban ministry has continued a claim on our lives. The above-mentioned suburban possibilities are incarnate in some people we know. Although they reside *in* suburbia, they are not *of* suburbia, at least as suburbia is conceived by its critics. They are models and mirrors of the new churchman, the new suburban-man, and the new hu-man.

If you asked us what they look like, sound like, and act like, our dossier on them would offer a composite image: suburbanites who are willing to shape their political and economic positions for the sake of justice for the entire metropolitan community; suburbanites who identify with the human revolution in its affirmation of dignity for all people everywhere; suburbanites who are uncompromising in their insistence on equality of opportunities; suburbanites who expect the church to be responsibly involved with social and political problems; suburbanites who believe in the expendability of present church structures in behalf of the mission.

To these persons who are the vanguard of suburban possibilities, and especially those with whom we have struggled to be the church in the congregations of Casa View United Methodist Church, Northaven United Methodist Church, and St. Stephen United Methodist Church, we offer these words as tribute and thanksgiving.

There is no human being who is who he is apart from the many gifts of community which have pollinated his personality, his ideas, his vision of life. For that reason any attempt on the part of authors to acknowledge their indebtedness to others is doomed to inadequacy. We owe much to our clerical colleagues, whose wisdom, faithfulness, and humanness have often sustained us in spite of our own blind spots and weaknesses. In this motley crew we include Tom Harris, Fred Gealy, Claude Evans, Ron Devillier, and Bob Cooper. We express our gratitude to Bishop W. Kenneth Pope, whose friendship has been a stimulus to our efforts as parish ministers. During all the years of our pastoral ministry, as well as during our seminary work, the faculty of the Perkins School of Theology has been a key resource, both in terms of personal relationships and intellectual challenges.

We owe a particular indebtedness to Dr. Schubert M. Ogden, who in the past dozen years has served us in a multi-faceted role as theological instructor, colleague and confidant, and more recently as scrutinizer of this manuscript. His incisive remarks were invaluable in reshaping and clarifying a good deal of the material. Whatever confusion and contradiction remain in the book are the fault of the authors alone.

To Mrs. Dotti Timmins we express our special gratitude for the typing of the manuscript (several times), and to Mrs. Marilyn Walker, Mrs. Robin Otstott, Mrs. Marge Lynn, and Mrs. Mary Lyman for related auxiliary work in the initial stages of manuscript preparation.

Saul Alinsky has said that there is no place better designed for reflective thinking and writing than in jail. This manuscript was not prepared in a jail setting, although if it had been, our task would have been completed much earlier and probably with greater precision. Considering the constant demands and responsibilities of the pastoral ministry, we began to suspect that anyone who could get out of the action long enough to write about it must surely be a phony. On the other hand, one could likewise suggest that anyone who could get out of the action long enough to read about it might also be a phony, and that would leave the authors in an embarrassing predicament!

PART I
mission interpreted

1
the new scene

A contemporary collage of the times does not make pleasant reading. Black manifesto. We had to destroy it in order to save it. The affluent society. Mass world starvation by 1980. What about our property values? Go to Vietnam, not to Cicero. White power. Pollution, strip mining, and disturbed ecology. Forty-nine Cong were bagged in the Mekong Delta. Supermarkets. The other America. They'll lower the educational standards. The guns of suburbia. Highly restricted. Campus disorders. They won't work. They're lazy. They're too ambitious. 47,159 American corpses.[1] Napalm. The resistance. Black Panthers. Russians keep out of Czechoslovakia. Green Berets. If they just wouldn't have so many children.

[1] Department of Defense Statistics, January 1, 1970.

Motorized America. Not old enough to vote. Old age. Illiteracy. Out of the national consciousness. Liberty and justice for all.

These synoptic signs tell us nothing new. They merely remind us of the conflicts which ceaselessly swirl around us like angry tidal waves. Out of the conflicts have come voices of dissent and discontent. Some of these voices are black. Some are white. Some are youthful. Others are poor. And some of them are suburban. The chorus of discontent has radically called into question our priorities and directions as a nation, a state, a city, a neighborhood, an individual.

A process of unparalleled soul-searching has been set in motion as a result of the sheer immensity of the national dilemma and the accompanying calls for reform. Although a polarization of viewpoints is taking place, so is widespread national analysis, including participation by individuals, committees, students, suburbanites, so-called experts, corporation boards, governmental agencies, and Congress.

A Root Problem: Suburban Priorities

What is happening is a clarification of the locus of our problems. The realization has begun to dawn that *the deepest causes* of our nation's ills are finally to be discovered not in the inner city, but in the attitudes and priorities of suburban man. For suburban ears this is a harsh claim, as we suburban authors can ourselves attest. The time may be late, but we suburbanites need to be asking in effect, "Is it I, Lord?"

If we open our eyes, we will discover that the distress and decay of the inner cities are symptoms of a deeper malady within the heart and soul of the white community. The black ghetto has become recognized as a disturbing mirror of who and what we have been as white suburbanites. The increasing awareness that suburbia is a root factor in the nation's disorders has made suburbia *a new scene*. It is a new missional scene because of our growing understanding that it constitutes the locale of major problems. The comic strip character Pogo said, "We have met the enemy, and they are we." This might well apply to suburbanites as we look at ourselves.

Too many of us in suburbia have demonstrated that only a special sphere of life, namely our own, has been important to us, and we have limited our responsibility to that same sphere. Neither suburban Christians nor those suburbanites who think of themselves as secularists are exempt from this judgment. There is a piece of many of us in the suburbanite who wrote the following letter to the *Dallas Morning News*:

In the Park Cities water board election on January 9, it was clearly indicated that Democrats, Republicans, and Independents, by a large majority did not want fluoridation of their water supply. They objected to a few people cramming something they did not want down unwilling throats. We are happy with everything as it is and want no changes made.

In the Park Cities we have excellent schools, fire and police departments, competent city councils and an excellent school board. Our insurance and taxes are lower. We have fine homes, higher property values, very few homes for rent or sale. Both Highland Park and University Park are run on a cash basis. Any indebtedness could be paid off with current taxes and our City Councilmen serve without compensation.

In this troubled world in which we live, there are wars and revolutions, . . . insurrections, mob violence, strikes, sit-ins, poverty, disrespect for laws and order in the U.S.A. None of these do we have in the Park Cities, and I believe that thinking citizens of these cities want to keep it this way.

Christ's Suburban Body

Everyone enjoys the beauty of the Turtle Creek area and of the Dallas Country Club and the convenience of our flourishing shopping centers. These suburbs are a credit to greater Dallas and may well be the inspiration for later developments within the city. The Park Cities truly provide the atmosphere for security, serenity, and satisfaction so dear to the homeowners' heart.[2]

Arnold Toynbee's research reveals that nation after nation has fallen by the wayside because of its refusal to involve itself in the welfare of all its people. But in spite of ample historical evidence to the contrary, somehow many suburbanites have deceived themselves into believing that they can flourish regardless of what goes on outside the suburban walls. When suburban man values his insulation and isolation so highly that he refuses to care about the well-being of others in the total community, he is actually sabotaging his own legitimate self-interests, at least in the long run.

If personal security is the limit of our aspirations we can be sure that whatever security we have in the affluent culture will be radically called into question. Piet Hein, the Danish poet, artist, and designer, memorably sums up what we are saying about the world today in one of his aphoristic poems known as "Grooks":

> Our choicest plans have fallen through,
> our airiest castles tumbled over,
> because of lines we neatly drew
> and lately neatly stumbled over.[3]

[2] January 24, 1968.

[3] From *Grooks* 1, by Piet Hein; © 1966 by Piet Hein; reprinted by permission of the author. *Grooks* 1 and 2 are published in the U.S. by Doubleday & Company, New York, and in Canada by General Publishing, Ltd., Ontario.

The New Scene

The advent and development of black power has been in particular one of the key factors in focusing on suburban attitudes as a source of national crisis. The welling up of a movement of self-esteem and self-consciousness in the black community has caused a crisis in belief for many of the basic presuppositions of the white community and its churches. Whites began to hear strange new words from the black ghetto. The word was—and the word is: The social problems of our nation are rooted in the attitudes and values of the white suburbanite. No longer can we deceive ourselves with analysis after analysis of what's wrong in the inner city. We are told to analyze our own community. Begin with yourself. Study yourself: your racism, your motives, your values.

In his book *Let's Work Together,* Nathan Wright, Jr., formerly Executive Director of the Department of Urban Work, Episcopal Diocese of Newark, New Jersey, suggests that although blacks must create their own power and identity, concerned whites can act as facilitators of efforts by black people to obtain legitimate power.[4] If the white community wants to do something about the riots and general unrest, it should look to itself for the answer. The basic task for whites of goodwill is to seek understanding and the spread of understanding.

Wright lists twenty tasks for white people, including (1) study your own historically rooted role in the vast amount of racism that exists in America today by (a) requiring that Negro and African history and culture be taught in our school systems at all levels and (b) encouraging church groups, cultural groups, and civic organizations to have series of discussions on American history in relation to black people so

[4] Nathan Wright, Jr., *Let's Work Together* (New York: Hawthorn Books, 1968).

21

that adults will also learn to understand themselves; (2) associate yourselves with thinking black people who accept their own blackness; (3) recruit and train better men to police our cities for the good of both white and black; (4) support programs for self-development of black people; (5) rethink job training and hiring policies in industry, business, and government.[5]

The *Report of the National Advisory Commission on Civil Disorders* (1968), commonly called the Kerner Commission, located the source of our national dilemma squarely in the hearts and minds of the white community. Cause and symptom were separated. The overt "troublemakers" caught in the act by TV may be the black rioters and those who advocate violence. The covert "troublemaker" wears a white mask and lives in the white "ghetto." The following is a quote from the summary report of the Kerner Commission.

> Certain fundamental matters are clear. Of these the most fundamental is the racial attitude and behavior of white Americans toward black Americans. Race prejudice has shaped our history decisively; it now threatens to affect our future. White racism is essentially responsible for the explosive mixture which has been accumulating in our cities since the end of World War II. Among the ingredients of this mixture are: (1) pervasive discrimination and segregation in employment, education and housing, which have resulted in a continuing exclusion of great numbers of Negroes from the benefits of economic progress; (2) black immigration and white exodus, which have produced the massive and growing concentrations of impoverished Negroes in our major cities, creating a growing crisis of

[5] *Ibid.* These five tasks are listed as examples of the twenty and are not numbered in Dr. Wright's order; see pp. 77-116.

deteriorating facilities and services and unmet human needs; (3) the black ghettos where segregation and poverty converge on the young to destroy opportunity and enforce failure.[6]

The American Party candidacy of George Wallace in the 1968 presidential election provided some statistical evidence for the attitudes of many suburban people. Eleven million votes cannot be lightly dismissed, nor can the future prospect of Wallace's candidacy. Revealing figures were also offered in the CBS Xerox-sponsored program, "Of Black America," especially in the last of the series in September, 1968. In a poll taken of a crosscut of white Americans, 49 percent said that in their opinion the Negro has not worked hard enough to obtain equality and that this was the main obstacle; 53 percent were of the opinion that Negroes tend to be lazier than whites; 40 percent said that Negroes have lower moral standards; and 48 percent objected to Negroes in all-white neighborhoods. The conclusion drawn by CBS programmers was that something like 35-40 million American whites could be classified as "racists." Not all of the whites interviewed were suburban residents, but the poll is indicative of the prevailing mind set within the suburban scene.

Of course, one does not have to be a poll watcher to be well aware of the racism which is so deeply embedded in our society. Whether you are making a retail purchase or talking to a neighbor, the blatant racism which so often crops up in conversation is a constant reminder of a sub-surface pathology which is widespread in our society. This pathology is especially seen in the unquestioned assumption that racist sentiments will not be challenged by those who hear these statements.

[6] Summary of Report (New York: Bantam Books ed., 1968), p. 10.

The well-documented study of the housing and educational integration of Teaneck, New Jersey, reported by Reginald Damerell in *Triumph in a White Suburb,* is a revelatory document for suburbanites. This community of 35,000 people struggled through years of conflict and crisis involving educators, churches, real estate agents, and a wide cross-section of the community. The 1965 school board election in Teaneck became the first local victory in the nation for integrated schools.

Damerell insists that only the most extraordinary confluence of favorable circumstances made possible the victory—a gifted and dedicated school superintendent, a couple of doctrinaire school board members who overplayed their hand in opposing integrated education, a sympathetic mayor, a civic conference which gave birth to a fair housing group and an advisory board on community relations, high caliber candidates and enthusiastic canvassers, an enlightened Jewish community, and the support of many clergymen. Damerell concludes: "Few whites anywhere will admit to racial prejudice, yet the continuing racial isolation all over the United States shouts to the heavens that the entire country is bristling with it. But if ever a community proved that the so-called 'Negro problem' is nothing so much as a 'white problem,' it is Teaneck." [7]

We have centered our attention mainly on the racial dilemma because, above all others, it clearly dramatizes the fact that suburbia needs to look in its own mirror. This does not mean that black people are without fault. To treat them as faultless would be a subtle form of dehumanization of both black and white citizens. It means, as more than one black person has

[7] *Triumph in a White Suburb* (New York: William Morrow & Co., 1968), p. 350.

said, that riots did not really begin in the streets. They began behind stained-glass windows and air-conditioned sanctuaries. Other social ills could have been used as evidence of the need for the reordering of suburban priorities and values.

A Root Possibility: Suburban Potential

Suburbia, we have suggested, is a new scene because we have awakened to the fact that it constitutes a root problem underlying our troubled times. Actually, we are speaking of a two-sided proposition. Suburbia is also a new scene because we likewise know it to be a repository of fantastic national potential.

Consider the situation. The vast majority of job opportunities are in the hands of whites. Except for creative innovations developed by the black community for its own people, public educational improvements must be mainly financed by suburban taxpayers. Financing of businesses in the black areas is often dependent on white sources. How can you upgrade slum housing when the landlords who hold the strings are white suburbanites? To reverse the conditions of unemployment or underemployment, poor housing and restricted housing, bad police relations, and insufficient education, white power is going to have to work with or for black power instead of against it. Until headway is made on the underlying causes of these inequities, the white man certainly cannot experience liberation of his own humanity, and the black man's dignity and freedom will be all the more difficult, if not impossible, to come by.

In terms of sheer numbers, suburbanites in 1964 constituted 60 million persons, or one out of every four Americans; by 1975 it is expected that one out of three Americans will reside in suburbia.[8] Lyle Schaller, pointing to a trend from urbanization to decentralization, says that in 1963, for the first time, the combined population of the suburbs exceeded the total population of all the central cities.[9] Even with the increase in the number of Negroes who manage to join the suburban ranks, the overwhelming majority of suburbanites is white.

Suburban potential, however, is more than numerical strength. Suburbia is ballot power. Collectively, the suburbanite has trained skills and the highest degree of formal education in the world. He is the possessor of technological and business know-how. His white power controls the money game. In spite of black power, white power is by far the dominant power in our nation. The question is, How will it be used? Can it be used in constructive ways?

Some critics of suburbia seem convinced that suburbanites, almost without exception, are seekers of refuge from minority groups, insistent on homogeneous neighbors, and possessed of forgetfulness of the "outside" world. Other analyzers of suburbia, writing from a pastoral and historical instinct, see the modern suburb as a coping device, at least in its origin. For example, Seward Hiltner believes the original impulse was basically a humane adaptation, namely, escape from the dehumanizing congestion, noise, and smoke of rising technology.[10] Without the exodus from the inner city, claims Hiltner, the result would have been far worse than today's situation. Once

[8] Frederick Shippey, *Protestantism in Suburban Life* (Nashville: Abingdon Press, 1964), p. 20.

[9] Schaller, *The Impact of the Future* (Nashville: Abingdon Press, 1969).

[10] Hiltner, "Troubled People in a Troubled World, People in the Suburbs," *Pastoral Psychology,* April, 1967, pp. 20-27.

established, however, the suburban areas became isolated and exclusive islands.

The truth is that suburbia means different things to different people. Suburbanites are not "lumpable" into a ncat, simplistic category any more than black people, poor people, or any other group of human beings. For many persons suburbia does serve as a tame life preserve, a protection, a privilege. For others suburbia offers housing advantages for a family, community services, supposedly some educational resources for children and youth, and recreational facilities. And some of the residents in every suburban community are passionately seeking to improve the living possibilities of *all* people.

Today there are thousands, perhaps millions, of second-generation suburbanites. They have not fled the inner city for either humane or selfish reasons because they have never lived in the inner city. They have never lived anywhere else but suburbia, or else they have migrated to suburbia from non-urban communities. These modern suburbanites constitute a potential in terms of self-development and future community development. The task of having even a minuscule part in enabling some suburbanites to reach out on behalf of the wider community will be neither simple nor particularly evident to very many people. It is not even possible unless we heed the words of Seward Hiltner: 'If you and I approach our suburb with condemnation, even with the Bible and sociology supporting us, we will not get very far." [11]

Suburbanites are frequently castigated for their apathy toward the misery and suffering of their inner city neighbors. Gibson Winter used the now wel-known term *amnesia* to

[11] *Ibid.,* p. 21.

describe the forgetfulness by which suburbanites shut out the world of human reality.[12] The truth of Winter's claim is inescapable, although we are not relieved of the responsibility of trying to understand the amnesia and deal with it constructively. Displaying little, if any, resistance to humane change in society, many suburban amnesia victims make no positive contributions either by word or by deed.

As Whitney Young has reminded us, the vast majority of whites show no ill will, but seldom do they show any concrete goodwill toward blacks. The apathetic suburbanite seldom votes in local elections, is poorly informed on what's happening, and is not involved in any program of continuing education. Actually he is a suburban "dropout" of our society, either not caring about responsibilities beyond his own needs or else seeing himself as a victim who can do nothing about the way things are.

The widespread apathy of many suburbanites may be intentional avoidance of involvement, but it is also an understandable concomitant of urbanization and technology. Complexity, specialization, mobility, and the population explosion all combine to erode the sense of personal responsibility of suburban man. Mobile psychology is the companion of mobile technology, creating a psychological distance as well as a geographical distance from the decision making process. The cerebral process often reasons like this: "By the time we take care of mere survival, a little time for family relationships and relaxation, who has time to decide the fate of the city, the nation, the world? We'll do well to manage the delicate balance of our own family and personal destiny, much less the fate of a wider community. We are a

[12] Winter, *The New Creation as Metropolis* (New York: The Macmillan Co., 1963), pp. 135-40.

society of specialists, so let the specialists do their thing. Why pour time and energy into local enterprises, whether church or school or political decisions, when we'll probably be living elsewhere in a few years anyway?"

Any chamber of commerce in an urban area can tell us the astronomical figures of new mobile immigrants pouring into the metropolitan area within any given week or month. The average figure for the city of Dallas is 345 new families per month. Here they come, rolling down the freeways. On the move. Uprooted. Anonymous figures whose ancestors were firmly planted in the familiarity of small town life. Urban nomads in a sea of strange faces. Start from scratch again. Locate the schools for the children. Find out where to shop for a thousand things. Where are the doctor's and dentist's offices? Which church for us? Put in a yard. School activities. PTA. Scouts and an array of other activities. Get the bills paid. And while you are at it, develop some family ties.

Once upon a time you were virtually assured of knowing how things were accomplished around town. You knew the school superintendent and school board members personally. Why, sure, the superintendent was old Sam who lived across the street with his wife and four kids and that scraggly hound dog. Now you have to make an effort to find out who the candidates are and where to vote, assuming you can even remember the proliferation of elections being held. Whereas in the old days it was a relatively simple matter to direct your political complaints to those who were in charge, in the new age the grievance mechanism is often complex and obscure. An appreciation for these factors is essential to an intelligent analysis of the suburban ministry and of suburban potential.

The suburban church does have a great deal of realizable

unfulfilled potential, as does suburbia itself. One of the claims of this book is precisely this fact. Apathy can be turned into concern, priorities can sometimes be changed, and power can be utilized in behalf of the oppressed and disadvantaged. And we should keep in mind too, as we will later, that the church is "in the business" of both personal care and social change. One of the reasons for pessimism and despair about the suburban church is that our expectations are either naïvely idealistic (result = despair) or else we belittle the real opportunities that are indeed in our midst (result = despair). Suburban potential, however, constitutes a basic possibility for the nation's future.

The Church and the New Scene

The recognition that suburban attitudes constitute a major source of social disintegration in this nation has not gone unnoticed by social reformers and churchmen. A new interest in "mission *to* suburbia" has been kindled with the hope that a reordering of suburban priorities will unlock new doors for the entire metropolis. The previous posture of "mission *from* suburbia" was usually not mission at all, but a condescending relationship to the inner city which actually prevented the likelihood of sweeping social changes.

In some cases there are dramatic shifts of emphasis from direct involvement with inner city problems to concern with suburban potential. One striking example of the changing scene from inner city to suburbia is the Institute for Middle Class Reformers instituted by Saul Alinsky in 1968. This school is a function of the Chicago-based Industrial Areas Foundation, which is noted for its Woodlawn Organization on Chicago's South Side. Representatives of the white middle class will be trained in the strategy of social revolution in the suburban context. Graduates are to return to their home bases as militant pressure group organizers. Plans call for the training of at least twenty-five organizers by early 1970, with subsidization for the first year coming from the Midas International Foundation.

When the initial announcement of the national institute was made, Alinsky observed that "lack of organization in white neighborhoods can be as harmful to the total society as lack of organization in the black community. We all live in our ghettos." [13] Who would have believed a year or two ago that the man more identified than any other in our country with inner city recovery would turn his attention to the suburbs? The new scene is where there is the most power to be organized.

Another mutation of direction is taking place in the model-building emphasis of the Ecumenical Institute in Chicago. For years the Institute poured its energy and resources into a comprehensive reformulation model for its Fifth City Project. Both on paper and in fact, in the abstract and the concrete, the Institute painstakingly created a viable plan for ghetto revitalization. It was offered as a model for inner city work throughout the United States.

In the summer of 1968 the Institute began to point with greater emphasis toward suburban recovery in its pedagogical courses and seminars. Suburban mission was no longer conceived as existing primarily for inner city involvement. The suburban scene had become a missional target in its own right. The Institute's gridding technique by which a geographical area is chosen and key problems sorted out was

[13] *The New York Times,* August 7, 1968.

applied to the ex-urban areas of the city. In addition, representatives of the Institute are now being dispersed throughout the nation in order to witness in suburban communities and churches.

The concept of the local church as an instrument for dealing with local problems is reflected in the following statement from an Institute working document. "The task of the Missional Parish is to provide community structures *within its boundaries* (italics ours) for equitable political participation by all residents, just economic provision for all residents, and adequate imaginal cultural symbols, education, and life style for all residents." Other Institute papers speak of an "in-but-not-of-suburbia" stance toward housing, financial resources, time, and corporate discipline. The essential point of these statements is that the mission thrust of the suburban congregation is seen as directed toward the root problem of which we have been speaking. In all likelihood the decision on the part of both Alinsky and the Ecumenical Institute to move into the suburban scene was "aided" by inner city militants.

In the local congregations of suburbia the context of ministry is facing a new day. If the task to be accomplished is described as "mission to suburbanites" in order to deal with basic problems of both inner city and suburbia, then an urgent significance is attached to the possibilities of the suburban ministry. Many clergymen have looked at suburbia as the fashionable promised land of success. Others have looked with understandable disdain on suburban ministry, believing that it was a phony protection from the suffering and deeper needs of powerless groups.

The challenge in suburbia may now in some ways be more difficult than the inner city ministry. The suburban resistance to change spells crisis and conflict for any minister who is even half serious about the gospel and the church's task. There aren't too many archconservatives in the inner city, but they are not lacking in suburbia. Inner city situations frequently are open to creative innovations and newly charted directions. The suburban ministry is more likely to be carried out amidst people who have definite notions about what they think the church should be and do.

If a pastor in the inner city clearly identifies with those who are in the greatest need, he is almost certain of acceptance and appreciation. Without denying the many legitimate needs of suburban church members, the suburban pastor who clearly identifies his ministry with the outcasts, the poor, black power, or the resistance movement can usually look forward to an exodus of members to "safer" churches, loss of financial support, internal congregational conflict, harassing phone calls, and possible walking papers.

Concern for suburban ministry has been an ascending priority on the drawing boards of the major denominations, but only for the past two or three years. For example, the Board of American Missions of the Lutheran Church in America is sponsoring a series of experimental conferences on suburban problems. Such matters as the suburban setting and psychology, social upheaval, and new methods of suburban church extension are under scrutiny. The United Presbyterian Council on Church and Race has established a new staff ministry to deal with white racism in the suburbs. The function of this ministry is to "help suburban people see how they are part of the problem of racism and what they can do about it." Entering the 70's Protestants will continue to shape new suburban strategies for the new missional frontier.

Although they may be a small percentage, there are awakened suburbanites who are deeply concerned and ready for action. They think and live beyond their own self-interests. They have come to believe, whether out of what we would call concern for others or out of enlightened self-interest, that shared power is the only power which can deliver us to a better future. They respect the function of law and yet know that law by itself cannot save our nation. They want to live in a cosmopolitan community. Knowing that their residence is changing within a year, they live their lives for maximum community benefit where they are. Knowing that they are only a few persons in an urban mass, they nevertheless do their thing in behalf of the total community. To develop and employ this awakened style of suburban living is perhaps the greatest challenge of the suburban church in the setting of the new scene.

A Sober Appraisal: Church Power and Suburban Power

The church, by faithfulness to the gospel and by wise deployment of its resources, can increase its effectiveness in the sphere of public responsibility, whether it be in the arenas of race, poverty, or other community problems. That's probably about as strong a statement as can be made by realistic appraisal.

With very few exceptions, the church is simply not powerful enough to single-handedly bring about sweeping social changes. By careful strategy and bold maneuvering, including propitious cultivation of both religious and secular allies, the church can have a hand in developing more humane possibilities for the metropolitan area. Later, we will be more specific as to types of homework which might be helpful, and actual implementation through task groups and ecumenical coalitions.

There is a very real sense in which one can challenge the idea that suburban power even exists. Writers like C. Wright Mills, in *The Power Elite* describe the immense power concentrated in corporations, the military system, political figures, and various institutions. One can then proceed to claim that suburban power as such is an illusion, or if it does exist, it is so diffused into complex and remote institutions that it is virtually beyond reach. Our purpose here is to recognize that there is at least a partial truth in these assertions. The seeming powerlessness of the masses has not escaped any of us.

However, there are forms of localized power residing within the suburban complex. There are educational systems, the matter of open housing, police-community relations, zoning ordinances, fair employment, human relations, and other issues which presuppose a decision-making process or the reality of power. These locally controlled forms of power are not beyond the probing and prodding of concerned citizens, including churchmen. Furthermore, there are signs that the basic trend in American society is a decentralization of power. When one ponders the Vietnam war, the Selective Service system, the heavy accent on military spending, or other policies, it is easy to fall into the trap of thinking that we are simply out of it. But even these can be challenged with some effectiveness over a period of time by concerned citizens throughout the country, and we have been seeing this happen to some degree in the past year or two.

At any rate, in *The Impact of the Future* Lyle Schaller provides some evidence that power in America is being divided among an ever increasing number of groups and organizations such as women, labor, blacks, students, the poor, and the consumer.[14] There seems to be some truth in his assertions, and

[14] Chap. 16.

this truth suggests that the church may realistically expect to play an important part in public responsibility if it desires to do so. There are, then, forms of suburban power which can be the subject of the church's concern and the target of its action. The church is by no means powerless. In fact, learning how to use its power strategically in God's mission is one of the essential and demanding tasks for the church of the 70's.

2
a theology of liberation

The Secular Meaning of the Gospel. The Secular City. God and Secularity. The Secularization of History. The Secular Christ. Secular Christianity. The Secular Congregation. The Secular Saint. By the time you read these words, the titles of these books concerned with today's church and culture will have been joined with others like them. *Secular Preaching. The Secular Sacraments. The Secular Word. Secular Means of Grace. The Secular Suburbs.*

The word "secular" (*saeculum,* of this present age) in its usage today points to two overriding and inescapable facts of our life and time, which account for its current dominance in theological thinking. (1) The world is viewed by contemporary man as man's task and responsibility. (2) The worth or significance of this world and our life therein is affirmed by modern man as ultimate and complete. No other world is needed to justify this one, and no one but man is expected to assume responsibility for the destiny and direction of our individual and common life. A theology for suburbanites in the 1970's will increasingly need to be geared toward the secular mind.

Yet these facts pose at least two key theological questions for the church today. Does the secular view of reality by its very nature presuppose an autonomous man who is in all respects independent from God? Or, may one embrace both the secular instinct for autonomy on the one hand and the biblical concept of accountability, obedience, dependence, partnership, and cooperation with God on the other hand?

The Gospel: Liberation for Accountable Autonomy

In his book *On Not Leaving It to the Snake,* Harvey Cox reminds us that sin can be interpreted to mean sloth and apathy as well as pride.[1] The implication is that man's being less than man (unwillingness to love the world and to take responsibility for it) is an insightful way by which to speak of the quintessence of sin in our time of history. When the church has spoken through the years of original sin, it has been pointing to man's constant substitution of himself in the place of God. However, original sin could also be interpreted to mean that human beings are forever selling their birthright of full humanity for some lesser status which is more comfortable or more easily obtainable.

The story of our lives is our ever-present tendency to give

[1] Harvey Cox, *On Not Leaving It to the Snake* (New York: The Macmillan Co., 1967).

our loyalties to gods or values not worthy of our ultimate trust; to feed ourselves with illusions and protective self-deceptions; to vacillate between pious self-congratulation on the one hand and depreciating self-pity on the other; to dehumanize our neighbor because of a vested interest which we allow to blind us; to wall ourselves off from the risks required of responsible men by the suffering around us; to hand over our own freedom to an assortment of powers and principalities which gladly relieve us of our selfhood.

Since the gospel is precisely that word which seeks to free men for their responsible autonomy in the world as authentic selves and as servants of justice and reconciliation, there is in reality no conflict between the claims of the gospel for man's accountability and the claims of secularity for man's autonomy. The point we have been striving to make is that man's condition is the fact of continually surrendering his autonomy for self and society or in countless ways avoiding the claims of that autonomy. Man's accountability of which the gospel speaks is an accountability for his true autonomy which he is ever forfeiting to some idea, purpose, or group.

On the surface, the biblical role of man's *accountability* seems to stand over and against the secular image of his *autonomy*. In scripture, man is viewed as one who tills the earthly garden as servant steward, who is called to obedience. The secular instinct, on the other hand, celebrates man's independence as one who is self-governed, his own decision maker, the determiner of his own destiny.

Far from being in insoluble conflict, however, these images of man actually reinforce one another and preserve an adequate view of man. Man cannot be accountable unless he has autonomy, for it is the just and humane use of his autonomy in the world for which he is accountable. Yet his autonomy is not self-created, nor is it responsible only to its own prompt-ings. Irresponsible accountability is also irresponsible au-tonomy, and vice-versa. Thus we may speak of autonomous accountability or accountable autonomy.

Autonomous accountability is neither an immature depen-dence on God nor an immature dependence on the world. The image of accountability preserves the fact that every man's life is a gift, that his life is only for a season, that his life is interdependent with other lives, that the style and direction of his life must be under constant review and renewal, and that prodigal use (or misuse) of his powers brings about harm to his neighbor and sabotage of his own true life. The image of autonomy, on the other hand, holds before us the reality that our lives require decision and risk, and that we cannot delegate our freedom to the control of others without sacrificing our true life. Both accountability and autonomy are not only truly biblical, but essential to true secularity as well.

If secularity were to be defined as love or responsibility for all of this world and all of this life, then we would be speak-ing of an understanding strikingly similar to the Christian gospel. Descriptive phrases such as holy worldliness, worldly holiness, Christian secularity, and secular Christianity are evidence of compatibility, if not identical viewpoints. Cer-tainly the Bible itself is no stranger to affirmations which sound like secular affirmations.

The very first chapter of Genesis affirms that the world is indeed man's task and responsibility. "And God said to them, 'Be fruitful and multiply, and fill the earth and subdue it; and have dominion . . . over every living thing that moves upon the earth.'" Furthermore, the worth of this world and the significance of man's life therein are likewise upheld. "And

God saw everything that he had made, and behold, it was very good." The Old Testament evolution of the prophetic message calling for individual responsibility and social justice pre-supposes man's responsibility for his world as well as the world's significance. We do not see the prophets calling men to an infantile dependence on God. They do not urge men to protect themselves and to escape the task of changing their society. We hear instead an Amos or an Isaiah calling men, in the name of God, to be liberated for autonomous accountability in the form of social justice.

There is a full orchestration of this liberating word throughout the New Testament. Whereas many persons have conceived of the gospel—with considerable assistance from the church itself—as a forfeiture of responsibility for oneself and the world, the gospel means exactly the opposite. Jesus is the embodiment of what it means to embrace this life and its people. His theme of liberation announces that men can truly live their lives in any and all circumstances, that the future given to them does not have to be determined by the past. Jesus is presented as an event through which men are confronted with the radical decision of whether or not they will accept God's gift of life as a good gift, the gift of accountable autonomy.

The Liberator: God

Earlier we commented that the secular mind posed two crucial theological questions for contemporary man. The first had to do with accountability and autonomy, which we have suggested are complementary terms. Together they provide a framework which does justice to the complexity of man's life and nature. The second problem is whether or not secular man can make any sense out of the term "God" and still be secular man. Before journeying further, it may be helpful to remind ourselves of two possible definitions.

In trying to relate secularization with Christian faith, some theologians have distinguished between *secularity* and *secularism*.[2] Whereas secularity is generally used to denote the outlook and methodology characterized by the attitudes of modern science, it does not insist that the scientific method is the only kind of valid knowledge. Therefore secularity, according to this definition, is not necessarily contradictory to Christian faith or its belief in God. Indeed, increasing numbers of Christian writers are going to great pains to show that their faith is a call to secularity, Harvey Cox being perhaps the foremost exponent, at least in the minds of many Christians.[3]

Secularism, on the other hand, is considered by the majority of theologians to be incompatible with Christian faith, or at least Christian faith in God, since secularism, according to this definition, restricts all knowledge to the principles of scientific verification. A theological position which supposedly theologizes without a belief in God—such as Paul van Buren's *The Secular Meaning of the Gospel*—claims no difficulty in embracing secularism into the essence of faith.[4]

In our own understanding, Christian faith and secularity are mutually compatible, in a similar sense that accountability and autonomy are complementary. While it is far from our intention to offer anything like a comprehensive doctrine of

[2] Schubert M. Ogden, *The Reality of God* (New York: Harper & Row, 1966), pp. 1-20.

[3] Cox, *The Secular City* (New York: The Macmillan Co., 1965).

[4] Paul van Buren, *The Secular Meaning of the Gospel* (New York: The Macmillan Co., 1963).

God, we would like to suggest an outline for the kind of theologizing which could responsibly reflect both scriptural fidelity and an entrée into the secular mind of today's suburban residents.

In English language the word "God" points to the unfolding, ongoing reality which provides us with a finite and free future, creating each new moment of time and life as a gift, and which at the same time calls us to use an accountable autonomy in shaping the future thus entrusted to us. It is no wonder that our Old Testament fathers spoke of this unfolding ongoingness (God) as the one sure fact of their lives. The unfolding ongoingness out of which came the future and its claim transcended and yet embraced everything that came into being. Political orders, empires, rulers, individual lives, human relationships appeared and disappeared, but the future-giving unfolding ongoingness continued. The Old Testament writers said that amidst all the uncertainties which swirled around their lives, one fact was absolutely clear; the unfolding ongoingness would continue to bring a finite future and demand that men shape that future for the well-being of all. God, for them, was this all-inclusive personal reality with whom they were confronted in every moment of life.

In this constantly emerging future, which is God's gift of himself, is the givenness of all that is. In this future all that happens happens. In this future all that comes into being comes into being, and all that passes away passes away. Only those who fail to appreciate what the biblical faith has meant by the word God can speak of the so-called death of God—unless they mean that the church has done such a poor job of interpreting God that God has virtually ceased to be a meaningful term for most secular men. To say that God is not, or is dead, is to say that no future is given and no claim is upon us. That is, life is *not*.

Indeed, our Old Testament fathers saw the unfolding, ongoing, creative process as a mysterious and marvelous epiphany, so that all of life was a showing forth, a manifestation, a revealing of God. They perceived the unfolding mystery of life not by use of scriptures, for they had none; not through church tradition; not through creeds and ready-made theological language; and not through the historical Jesus. Through experience of life itself they developed a vocabulary to describe what they experienced, issuing forth ultimately in scripture, tradition, creeds, and the like.

For men like Amos, Isaiah, and Jeremiah, God talk did *not* mean some questionable object out there or up there. God language was their way of pointing to the ongoing, unfolding reality of the way things come and go in all of their depth and mystery. This unfolding, ongoing reality addresses men with a personal epiphany of judgment and mercy through the events of life, meaning that in all events there is a creative, saving possibility given. It is not surprising that in the third chapter of Exodus God says to Moses, in reply to the question about God's name, "I am who I am," or as some scholars have interpreted it, "I am the One who brings to pass that which comes to pass." We can call this reality the way things are, the way it is, all that is, what's happening, the never-ending, all-inclusive, unfolding ongoingness, or God. But whatever we call it, one thing is absolutely certain. It is. It was. It will be. It is unceasingly offering man a future and calling him to the liberation of accountable autonomy through which to shape this future.

Our fathers also claimed that the God epiphany—the unfolding ongoingness of all that is—is always the same, yet never the same. The unfolding ongoingness is in one sense always the same, addressing men as judgment and love, offering the liberation to live their lives in accountable autonomy. On the other hand, God is never the same, coming to men as new in every event, unique and unrepeatable. This is the way it was in the beginning, is now, and ever shall be, world without end.

A similar way of talking about the unfolding ongoingness of all that is, is to say that this reality is change or social process. The totality of change our fathers perceived as the Love of God, because out of it came all the possibilities that are given. They saw that everything is subject to the process of time and decay except the reality of process itself. All life was and is unceasingly subject to the law of process and change.

Implicit in our fathers' faith was the realization that life's meaning, its potential and possiblity, is dependent on the fact of change. No change means no life. Without change there would be only a frozen, static form. Life could not come into being because that very coming is process or change. Life presupposes change, growth, process. Therefore, in spite of the anxiousness and uncertainty caused by change, our fathers saw that the fact of change, that is, the unfolding ongoingness of all life, was their best friend, the giver of all possibility. Therefore, they called this reality "Father," since it gave birth to all that has been, is, and could become. The totality of change they called the Love of God, because in and through this totality, the all-inclusiveness of change, they discovered their own meaning and significance.

They saw change, with all of its implied threats, as the inevitable one and only condition out of which life could evolve. In the totality of change they lived, and moved, and had their being. Their own being was temporal, yet forever a part of the unfolding, ongoing reality of change. The purpose of a liberating, accountable autonomy, according to our fathers, was not the elevation of men to the status of supreme being, but rather the freeing of men to live their lives in a manner that celebrated the worth of the unfolding, ongoing epiphany of life known as God. To live for any lesser reality was not really to live, but to exist in bondage.

Our fathers observed that somehow the past is always being received, and a new future being offered to us, so that the possibility of living our lives in spite of all the "in spite ofs" of life is always being given. This reality comes from God, and is a sure sign that the fundamental truth of existence is love. Whereas a great deal of theology shoves God out of the real experience of men, making him unreal or "dead" in the understanding of secular man, biblical theology speaks of God in the judgments which life invariably thrusts upon us and the forgiveness or new future which we are always being offered by the unfolding ongoingness of life. Biblical theology tells it *the way life undeniably is,* and is therefore a *reality theology*.

It is understandable that from time to time we may wish the death of this unfolding ongoingness who lays his claim upon us. Those who have never wished for the death of God have never comprehended what biblical faith means by the word "God." The cross is an eternal reminder of man's wish for the death of the ongoing one who lays upon us a claim to give up our illusions for reality, our self-protection for risk in the world, our vested interests for a universal concern. The incarnate representative of the unfolding, ongoing reality was slain, but the future is still created with its promises and demands. Although Luther may not have so intended, he was summarizing the Easter faith in his great phrase from "A

46

Mighty Fortress Is Our God"—"The body they may kill; God's truth abideth still."

The Gospel: Liberation for Selfhood

The gospel is being before doing, who am I before what do I do, personal before it is political. This means that the word of liberation calls us to the freedom to be ourselves. Even the much-needed insights of social change theologies must not be allowed to obscure this emphasis. Our freedom is grounded in our birthright; that is, our value and significance as human beings are intrinsic in our very birth. We cannot earn or prove our worth. We can only come to a greater awareness that we already have a birthright of dignity and worth as a gift from the unfolding ongoingness out of which all that is given is given.

This birthright is not the gift of the state, the society, the economic or educational system, or even our parents. Any of these may impede or distort our awareness of our worth as persons. On the other hand, as agents of transmission they may equip us to recognize our uniqueness as persons. An infant is worth loving and learning to love because he already possesses the birthright of a human being. The liberating word tells us that we belong not to the state, to the system, to the group, or to any other person. Nor do we belong finally to any dehumanizing idea about ourselves which has been transmitted to us by others. We belong to God, the reality out of which our past is received, the future is given, and from which comes the demand to become a self of accountable autonomy. The gospel is that word which says to us, "You are valued for yourself." Virtually every other word says, "You'll be valued if you join my movement, or if you will do my thing."

The freedom to be ourselves, that is, to receive our lives as being good as given, implies the freedom to live in the now. Until we accept ourselves within the context of our givenness, we are prone to live in the past or in the future. Unable to accept the negations of our existence, we live in a "what if" world instead of the "what is" world. The freedom to be ourselves suggests the freedom to prefer reality to illusion.

The freedom to be ourselves implies the freedom from ultimate dependence on the outcome of any personal or social endeavor, no matter how worthy or good. In Charles Schulz's delightful book of teen-age cartoons entitled *What Was Bugging Ol' Pharaoh?* there is a scene in which a teen-age boy is preparing to unleash his bowling ball down the lane. He is saying to his girlfriend, "I can't seem to get a strike to save my soul, but fortunately the salvation of my soul doesn't depend upon my getting a strike." [5]

Many persons in our day seem to make their lives depend on the outcome of some particular individual or social goal. If our lives are ultimately dependent on anything other than the liberating word itself, the word will address us as the word of judgment. That judgment will come upon us as fear of the future and the fear of being ourselves. Conversely, the reception of the word is a freeing experience enabling us to receive the gift of a free self facing a new future.

The freedom to be ourselves implies the freedom to decide the direction and destiny of our own lives. Either we attempt to take responsibility for our lives, or we turn our lives over to someone else. In the latter case, when things go wrong we can blame those to whom we have turned over our lives. Remember? Adam blames Eve. Eve blames the serpent. The question

[5] Charles M. Schulz, *What Was Bugging Ol' Pharaoh?* (Anderson, Ind.: Warner Press, 1964).

posed by the word of liberation is, "Who's going to live your life—you, or someone else?" The gospel is a revolution in self-understanding and in social understanding because it constantly judges systems and relationships which prevent the emergence of dignity and responsible self-direction. Again and again we see in our experience as pastors the need of suburban man to receive himself as a self, not as property of a corporation, not as condemned because of his past, not as one who need live in fear of change.

The liberating word about life, strangely symbolized in the cross, claims that we can live only by dying, that we must die to whatever keeps us from living our lives. And so to the Pharisees from Jesus: die to your religion of legalistic rules so that people can become more significant in your sight than your codes and laws about people. To those who covet recognition for their actions: die to your craving for attention, so that you can find joy in life and in yourself. To those who cannot live today for worrying about tomorrow: die to your self-imposed prison so that you can be free for today. To those who are obsessed with the need to be right: die to your phony self-image so that you can be yourself for once. Die to the constant blaming of others, to wishing you were somebody else, to wishing for some other set of circumstances, to intoxicating yourself with pipe dreams, to waiting for some miracle ship to come in and save your life, so that you can begin to live now.

The freedom word comes as both a sentence of death and a summons to life. There can be no newness in our being, no freedom to struggle with our past or our present, except by way of dying. And that is the undeniable truth about life of which the cruciform word is the eternal reminder. As an instrument of death it says to us, "Die so that you can live." And this means change.

As a matter of fact, one way to describe the function of Jesus as the Christ is to say he is God's change agent, calling men to die to their false securities and to give themselves to a trust in life and a new care for others. At the state or county fair, have you ever watched the ride on the midway in which the customer rides a conveyor-like belt to the top of the platform and then slides down a curling, twisting slide? In some places this ride is called the "cakewalk" (not to be confused with the better known game of that name where cakes are given as prizes). If you have watched this modern midway cakewalk, you have seen a parable of the Christ function as understood in a real Christian theology.

As the customers, usually children and youth, step onto the conveyor-like cakewalk belt, they try desperately to hold on to the sides in order to protect their footing and their upward journey on the cakewalk. The more they grasp and clutch the rail, the more impossible their situation becomes. The more they try to reduce their vulnerability by holding on to the rail, the more vulnerable they become, slipping, sliding, and frequently collapsing. The choice which appears to be most secure and most supportive (holding on to the rail) in reality turns out to be the least secure. Their only hope is to surrender their supports and trust the conveyor-like cakewalk.

As you watch them clinging and slipping and sliding, you will rarely see a single one who, of his own accord, decides to trust the cakewalk (unless he has learned this by previous trips on the cakewalk). The function of the cakewalker, usually a young man employed by the cakewalk, is to urge, coax, and sometimes almost literally pull the struggling person from his false support and place him on the cakewalk so he can ride it in his own newfound freedom up to the top. The look of surprise and even exhilaration on the faces of those who are liberated from their false supports, and who discover they can trust the cakewalk, is truly a beautiful sight. (Try it next year at the fair.)

In this parable of the cakewalk, we see a paradigm of the Christ function to liberate us from our false securities for a new future of trust and confidence. We do not "save" ourselves, yet the cakewalker (Christ) does not shelter us or live our lives for us. He is the agent of care who offers to free us from our false crutches and for autonomous adventuresome life (to be ourselves). Whenever this freeing event offers itself to us as a new possibility, we experience the liberating confrontation of which Jesus as Christ is the ultimate definition. He is the model of God's liberating mission.

The Gospel: Liberation for Others

The gospel of liberation is not only a personal freedom to be oneself, but also the capacity to be free for others. Indeed, to truly be oneself means also the freedom to be for others. Liberation is liberation for God's mission, whatever specific form it may take in the life of a given human being. Furthermore, being free for others presupposes both giving and receiving. Usually we think of the Christian ethic in terms of doing for others, bearing their burdens, meeting their needs, whether in a personal or a social context. We should remember that being free for others also means freedom to receive from them. Unless parents can receive from their children, unless white culture can receive from black culture, then all concerned are being cheated. If we only give but don't receive, we are dehumanizing those to whom we give, as well as ourselves.

Many times those who are weak in terms of worldly power

and advantages have much to give to those who are strong in worldly terms. These should not be strange words to persons who have acquainted themselves with biblical insights, but they are words we suburbanites desperately need to hear. For example, in I Corinthians we are told: "God chose what is foolish in the world to shame the wise, God chose what is weak in the world to shame the strong, God chose what is low and despised in the world, even things that are not, to bring to nothing things that are."

There have been many times in history when the so-called weak in society have been bearers of truth to those who are strong in position and power. Essentially this was the story of the early church. When the establishment is called into question, it is frequently by the disadvantaged minorities and the disquieting voices of youth who are demanding an audit of the existing system. In sometimes being bearers of the truth to those who are in power, the disinherited reveal what it means to be more fully human.

Being free for others inevitably propels us into the social dimension of the gospel of liberation. For the word is not only about personal freedom, but is likewise the insistence that we be about the task of freeing others. The liberated man will join the movements of his time which are working for the liberation of others. The free men of every generation are to become agents of change in order to "bring good tidings to the afflicted, . . . to bind up the brokenhearted, to proclaim liberty to the captives, and the opening of the prison to those who are bound, to proclaim the year of the Lord's favor and the day of vengeance of our God, to comfort all who mourn" (Isaiah 61:1, 2). Currently, this would suggest the liberating of white suburbanites from the dehumanization of their mental ghettos and the freeing of minorities and poor from the dehumanization of their second-class status.

Implications for the Church

The church could well be defined as a word-bearing community, bending and expending itself on behalf of the humanness of all men. Whatever the shortcomings of this shorthand definition may be, there are two crucial points which it clearly expresses. For one thing, the church is defined as a community which bears a word about life. God's liberating word of accountable autonomy for oneself and for others constitutes the foundation, the motivation, and the guiding motif for the church's existence. Without this word, the church is reduced to simply another action-oriented organization. The uniqueness of the Christian community is rooted in its task of being a word bearer. No other organization, institution, or community exists for this particular function.

At the same time, the remainder of the definition calls to our attention that the church is rightly a militant shepherd risking itself in a servant style of life and called to join God's liberating work in the world. In other words, when the word that God is at work in his world to liberate men is actually incarnated in the world, shaped as justice and love for neighbor, reincarnation Christian style has taken place.

There is a sense in which the church belongs in the hell of the world. These are almost terrifying words to many suburbanites, but they contain the seeds of liberated life. The life decision of greatest magnitude for both individuals and congregations is whether we will isolate and insulate ourselves as dropouts from the needs of others, or else choose to care, to feel, to hurt, to risk for others. The parable of the Last Judgment in Matthew 25 is an unforgettable statement about what counts most in life. We are told that it is in meeting the needs of the hungry, the outcast, the poor, that we encounter life's ultimate meaning. And we find this meaning—the real, the true, the ultimate—in the last place imaginable. Not in provincial life styles, not in technology itself, not in affluence of goods and things, not in control of others, not in our rating with society. We find "the real" in the struggle for humanness, in the agony and the ecstasy of the collision between God's word and God's world.

It follows that in the hell of the world we likewise discover our own humanity, our own true selves. There is irony and surprise in the fact that we cannot find lasting peace apart from concern for others. In affirming others, we affirm ourselves. We discover in humanity's hell a sense of purpose, an identity, a courage, a cause, a self. A college professor said to a group of students that naturally God seemed unreal to those whose greatest concern was which fraternity to choose or what the next hairdo would look like. He invited them to become real by investing their lives in the struggle for peace and justice.

It is strange that Christianity has traditionally interpreted heaven as a comfortable refuge in the presence of God and hell as a place of suffering apart from God. Everything about the life and cross of Jesus makes the point that we find God in the suffering of his people because that's where he is revealing himself as comforter and liberator. If we were to pretend that the orthodox interpretation of heaven and hell were true, then we'd really find God in hell, comforting his people and ministering to their wounds and hurts. And there would be Jesus—he descended into hell—distributing the bread of renewal. The Bread Man cometh even into hell! The church's task is to join him there as witnessing servant.

The ministry of Jesus may be described in part as the commissioning of his followers to enter into hell, that is, the suffering and the hurt and injustices of the world, the world for which God is acting and caring through the gift of a future and the always-present demand for love and justice. In Mark 5 when the Gerasene demoniac begged to go with Jesus in the boat following his healing, Jesus said in effect, "Go to hell." He was really telling him to go back to his community where life is, where people work and agonize and suffer and die, and minister to them.

Perhaps in addition to the time-honored greeting of "grace and peace," we in the Christian community should be saying to each other, "In the name of Jesus Christ, go to hell"—to where principalities and powers are robbing men of their humanity, into the suffering, the humiliation, the injustices of the world where God is at work freeing the captives. "He descended into hell" in the Apostles' Creed is a much-needed reminder of a missional style of life held before us in Christ.

Historically, whenever the church has gone through a metamorphosis from a servant, pilgrim people to a powerful, triumphalist institution; when the church manipulated the poor into bearing the burden of supporting ostentatious cathedrals instead of the church caring for the poor; when the church's image became that of a property holder instead of a vulnerable servant of mankind;—the church ceased being the church at its best. The erosion of the cruciform style of life was the emasculation of the church's reason for being. When the church has been a faithful community, it has recognized vulnerability as the life style necessary for the creation of justice and liberation. Social progress is hammered out on the human anvils of those persons who are willing to become the vulnerable ones of history, the risk-takers who enter the hell of the world with whatever resources and power they can muster.

A recent Associated Press report told how 2,000 black and white high school students in New Brunswick, New Jersey, joined by city and school officials, marched in the streets with arms linked in a display of racial unity. Many of the faculty cried openly, overcome by the display of racial and human solidarity. The unity march followed on the heels of fighting between black and white pupils which had caused the school to be closed for two days to allow a "cooling off." The idea for the integrated march came from a small group of pupils of both races.

We know the identity of this small group of students. They are the avant-grade of history, the human anvils, the vulnerable ones who risk themselves in word and deed for the good of humanity. That's who we of the suburban church are called to be—a word-bearing community, bending and expending ourselves in behalf of the humanness of all men, and asking nothing in return.

To give expression and implementation to the theology of personal and social liberation is the practical test of the church. We cannot settle for one at the expense of the other. The church's competent theologians have always recognized that the gospel is both a promise of personal liberation and a demand to free others as a visible sign of that liberation. Indeed, these cannot be separated. Promise without demand is what Bonhoeffer called "cheap grace." It is the revivalistic "my God and I" theology which, unlike biblical theology, is not neighbor-oriented. On the other hand, demand apart from promise is at best a half gospel. The peculiar temptation of a theology of social change is to concentrate on God's activity in political events to the exclusion of a personal gospel concerned with the universal human condition of guilt, anxiety, and death, and the universal human need for acceptance, joy, and understanding,

If theology is to energize the faith community instead of crippling it; if God language is to point to the realities of our existence instead of to hypothetical and theoretical maybes; if theology is to gain the respect of the secular suburbanite rather than limp along as a dead language used by the compulsively religious; then the language of theology must express itself in a style of Christian secularity and the content of theology must push the church into the hell of the world as a vulnerable servant community.

The proper function of theology in the local church—whether in proclamation or in group study and reflection—is to oil and grease the runways leading to accountable and autonomous selves in the world; to nourish relationships with a ground of grace; to set the mood and style for the life of the faith community; to enable people to sort out an overall picture of life's purpose and destiny; to facilitate the celebration of the worth of life in all circumstances; and to bring to the surface the subterranean courage and hope which are present in every human life. It is in these directions and for these purposes that we are pointing when we speak of the proper task of theology today in its more formal and systematic sense: "to bear witness in the most adequate conceptual form now possible to the reality of God which is re-presented to us all in Jesus Christ." [6]

[6] Schubert M. Ogden, *The Reality of God*, p. 70.

3
a fourfold missional design

Theologians seem to be endowed with an innate propensity to think in trinitarian terms. The classical Christian doctrine of God has been expressed through a threefold prism. The seasons of the church year, at least in one common arrangement, revolve in a threefold cluster, pointing to examination or expectation, joyful victory, and a sending forth to commitment (Advent-Christmas-Epiphany, and Lent-Easter-Pentecost). Many orders of worship reflect a threefold sequence in terms of the Service of Confession, the Service of the Word, and the Service of Commitment. Preaching in Protestant circles seemed to be dominated for years by a triadic arrangement of the homily.

It does not surprise us, then, when we see that the church has utilized a threefold norm to describe the functions which freight its theology into the world. At least this seems fair to claim from the standpoint of contemporary retrospection, using biblical terms with which to summarize the church's past. The functions are the ways and means by which the church fulfills its reason for being, namely, to bear witness to the liberating mission of God in the world. An interesting assortment of terms and labels has been used from time to time to interpret these functions, but nearly always the conclusions have been framed within a threefold formula.

The New Testament provides a ground for the missional thrust of the church in the pattern of Jesus' own ministry. Particularly fascinating in this respect is the Gospel according to Mark. This Gospel theologian wastes no time in revealing the activities of calling, healing, and feeding as constituting the liberating work of Jesus. The proclamation that the Kingdom of God is at hand is the first public act of Jesus' mission. Next is the particularization of the proclamation, as Simon and Andrew, and then James and John, are called. The calling is followed by a healing of the man with an unclean spirit and of Simon's mother-in-law. In Mark 6 and 8 we are offered the feeding accounts in which it is said of the people, "They ate and were satisfied." A rotation of the threefold theme is Mark's theological model for presenting the significance of Jesus and his work.

Students of Mark's Gospel have called our attention to the Old Testament sequence from which Mark surely drew his new covenant scenario. In the Exodus narrative the themes of calling, healing, and feeding stand out. The people are called out of bondage by God's liberator, Moses. God raises up his people for a new future, and brings them through the Red

Sea and subsequent dangers on all sides. In the wilderness they are fed with the heavenly manna. In a sense, the entire biblical story is one of God calling his people to a liberated life, healing them with the cleansing forgiveness of a new future, and sustaining them through any and all circumstances of life.

A summation of Jesus' ministry is offered in Mark 3. "And he appointed twelve, to be with him, and to be sent out to preach and have authority to cast out demons." From this kind of source material the church's theologians have derived the interpretation of the church's mission in terms of *kerygma,* *koinonia,* and *diakonia.* The kerygmatic function is the activity of proclaiming or preaching, the public announcement of what God is doing in the world and how we may become partners in his liberating action. The koinonia function points to the relationship of members of the faith community with one another, sharing in common the gifts and risks of Christian discipleship. Koinonia is an expression of loving acceptance in human relationships, a community of care and concern for one another, shaped around the image of Christ. The diakonia function refers to the role of the church as the servant reconciler and healer. Some churchmen limit the meaning of diakonia to care or outreach to individuals, whereas other interpreters would include the entire range of the church's function as an agent of social change and servant of justice.

Functions: Contemporary Reinterpretations

It is instructive to notice how contemporary writers have reshaped these three missional functions with a variety of nuances. In an article entitled "The Responsibility of the Church for Society," Richard Niebuhr made use of the threefold formula by describing the functions of the church in terms of apostle, pastor, and pioneer. The church is an apostolic community existing for the sake of announcing the gospel. With an awareness of the immediate moment and its needs, the apostolic messenger announces the gospel to both individuals and nations. As pastor, the church serves as shepherd of the sheep, seeker of the lost, friend of publicans and sinners, and of the poor and brokenhearted. The pastoral concern for individuals leads to responsibility on the collective level as well.

In the third image, of pioneer, the church was envisioned by Niebuhr as the social trailblazer who carves out new images and models in behalf of humanity. The Christian community pioneers in repentance and reformulation of society. "As the representative and pioneer of mankind, the church meets its social responsibility when in its own thinking, organization, and action, it functions as a world society undivided by race, class, and national interest. In pioneering and representative action of response to God in Christ, the invisible church becomes visible, and the deed of Christ is reduplicated." [1]

In *The Secular City*, Harvey Cox reclothes the kerygmatic function of the church by calling it "broadcasting the seizure of power." The church is the signaler who flashes the news that the revolutionary change agent is at his task of freeing men from bondage. The hearer receives a concrete invitation to join the struggle. "Healing the urban fractures" is Cox's way of talking about the diakonic function. The healer must know the wounds of the city, as well as how to join the

---

[1] Niebuhr, "The Responsibility of the Church for Society," in *The Gospel, the Church, and the World*, ed. Kenneth Scott Latourette (New York: Harper & Row, 1946), pp. 111-33.

healing process already under way through God's initiative. The church's koinoniac function is making visible the city of man, that is, a visible demonstration of what the church is saying in its kerygma and upholding in its diakonia.

Yet another design for the threefold mission appears in Stephen Rose's *The Grass Roots Church*.[2] The triadic arrangement is laid out by picturing the church in terms of chaplaincy, teaching, and abandonment. Under chaplaincy, Rose visualizes the spectrum of worship, preaching, and pastoral care. Generally speaking, the ordained leadership of the priestly, liturgical, kerygmatic ministry of the church is included in the chaplaincy function. Teaching, the second function, is seen as an assignment best handled through ecumenical specialization. Abandonment implies the servant community with a cruciform style of self-giving. It means a giving up of one's self to a task in behalf of others.

Functions: Parish Pragmatics

Thus far we have suggested the functions of the church's mission by pointing to the norms which seem to have arisen from the gospel itself, or at least the traditional interpretation of its implications. There is another method, however, by which we can view the church's functions. If we examine the mission from the standpoint of a pragmatic description rooted in the practical work of the parish, we could authentically speak of a fourfold division instead of the historic trinitarian arrangement. The fourth task is teaching (pedagogy, instruction, reflection), known traditionally as *didache*.

Over thirty years ago C. H. Dodd, a British New Testa-

[2] Stephen C. Rose, *The Grass Roots Church* (Apex. ed.; Nashville: Abingdon Press, 1966).

ment scholar, developed an argument for a sharp distinction in the New Testament between kerygma and didache, between preaching and teaching. Since that time other scholars have, in our judgment, refuted Dodd's case by showing that kerygma and didache may both include theological proclamation and ethical instruction.[3] Didache, in their view, is a special mode of preaching the gospel, so that there is no clear-cut distinction between the church's preaching and teaching ministries.

Recognizing this fact, we can proceed to say that in the actual designing of the church's work on the local level, we are speaking of two distinct disciplines. Most of us recognize this fact in the church's organizational structure, and have done so for years. For example, in a United Methodist congregation, the Commission on Worship is one responsibility, and the Commission on Education is quite another, because the disciplines of planning require a separation of functions.

Thus, the fourfold functions of worship, education, community, and action seem to summarize the mission of the church from the standpoint of practical design. *Worship,* which is basically the celebration of the worth of life, includes the priestly role of administering the sacraments, plus weddings and funerals, which are properly understood as services of worship. *Education* embraces all programming of classes, academies, forums, seminars, and study groups, and, except in very small congregations, needs to be subdivided into children, youth, and adult work. *Community* points to encounter groups, house churches, pastoral care, and other methods projected to enable persons to come alive to themselves and others. It is a judgment on the Christian community when the

[3] Victor Paul Furnish, *Theology and Ethics in Paul* (Nashville: Abingdon Press), 1968, pp. 98-111.

lack of real community leads a member of the congregation to say, "This congregation is the loneliest part of my world." Today's human potential movement, perhaps at least partially symbolized by William Schutz's book *Joy* (Grove Press, 1967), has made the church more aware of the deep needs for community in today's depersonalized urban culture. *Action* or engagement of society refers to the servanthood of the church in the wider community, either by ministering to the needs of individuals or by involvement in social issues.

Before proceeding, we must mention still another function which probably should change this chapter title to "A Fivefold Missional Design." Many churchmen would place it not only on our list of practical functions in the local parish, but as number one. *Evangelism.*

In a way, evangelism is the most inclusive, since all of the church's functions constitute a witness to the liberating mission of God in the world. It has been said many times that the church does not have a mission, it *is* mission. Similarly, the church does not perform evangelism, it *is* evangelism. It is a community which is called to be Word bearing and world bearing, pointing beyond itself to the ultimate worth of the unfolding ongoingness of all that is (God). Because of evangelism's inclusive nature, there is nothing about the church that is not evangelism insofar as the church is a faithful community, and so we have not included it in our functional design.

However, there is a narrower sense of evangelism which especially invites inclusion. There is the quite important task of the suburban church reaching out to persons in the residential area by way of informing them of the presence, care, and work of the congregation, and inviting them to participate in the mission. A congregation unconcerned at this point is not keeping faith with its responsibility to the community, and it is jeopardizing the maximum effectiveness of its own mission. We are not concerned here to elucidate ways and means by which this kind of evangelism is accomplished, whether by one-to-one confrontation, by mass communication, or by a small group method. Rather, we wish to affirm the legitimacy of true concern for people which is the heart and soul of the church's evangelism.

Returning now to the fourth function, or action, we may note Peter Berger's suggestive picture of the church's relationship to society. He speaks of Christian engagement of society, and outlines four major possibilities of such social engagement, which we have paraphrased.[4]

1. *Christian diaconate*—"the helping outreach of the Christian community to individuals in distress—those suffering from illness, poverty, or other personal difficulties." This emphasizes the primary importance of unspectacular and unpretentious Christian concern for the unique individual in his unique needs.

2. *Christian action*—"any attempt not only to deal with individuals but also to try to modify the social structure itself." Such action will try to induce social change in some direction thought desirable from the viewpoint of Christian ethics.

3. *Christian presence*—"the erection of Christian signs in the world." This is an identification with suffering where other recourses of social change are not possible, as in a suppressive state. An example would be voluntarily living

[4] Peter Berger, *The Noise of Solemn Assemblies* (Garden City, N. Y.: Doubleday & Co., 1961).

among the poor, sharing their suffering where no other recourse is available.

4. *Christian dialogue*—"the attempt to engage the Christian faith in conversation with the world." Whereas Christian action (#2 above) depends on a diagnosis of the situation that isolates certain facts or events as morally untenable and then proceeds to eliminate or modify them, Christian dialogue functions as a facilitator of communication between parties in more complex ethical situations.

By now the reader may be asking himself, "What difference does all this terminology make in actual practice?" It is a good question, and we believe there is an important answer.

The labels themselves are not particularly important, except as they help to clarify our vision of the whole. There is no religious "circumcision" in the choice of nomenclature. The labels do remind us of a matter that occasionally seems to escape the attention of churchmen on both the left and the right: the mission of the Christian community is not reducible only to what happens when the congregation gathers, nor only to what happens when the congregation is scattered in the world.

Churchmen on the right have too often seen the mission almost solely in terms of what goes on within the church building, or else the activity outside the building carried on in order to get more people inside the building. Social activists on the left have been tempted to use social witness as the sole criterion for the validity of the church. For them, proclamation, teaching, and community have been either largely insignificant or else demoted to the second-class status of "preparation for mission."

A little reflection enables us to recall the danger of unwarranted reductionism. Without social engagement or action, worship and education are likely to become exercises in escape from the world, instead of a call to participate in God's mission in the world. The word, truly preached and taught, and the sacraments, duly administered, confront us with worldly decisions. The world is weary of a church that does not incarnate its creeds with deeds. If we say we love God, but neglect our neighbor, then we are liars.

But it is just as true that commitment to social action can become inhuman or distorted, as we have seen in many revolutions, without a judging and cleansing word. Social action can become an idol without the liberating word, which reminds us that our lives do not finally depend on the outcome of any specific missional task or combination thereof. When social action becomes the all-in-all, despair is likely to be lurking around the corner.

Some of the most exciting happenings going on in local churches today are small encounter groups through which persons are enabled to experience the reality of a loving, caring commmunity. *This is God's mission.* A wide variety of communications media—tapes, films, banners, posters, personal encounter, dance, records, drama, role playing—plus the emphasis on celebration and joy have reclaimed worship as a truly life-giving experience for many congregations. *This is the mission of God.* Education, too, is making use of self-directed study groups, case studies, and sensitivity training in order to equip persons for the gospel, both personally and politically. *This is mission.*

Pastoral and lay care of human beings in personal distress is also mission. Listen to Peter Berger in *The Noise of Solemn Assemblies:* "There are some Christians whose one vocation remains to suffer and to face death in faith. It is certainly no minor accomplishment if a local congregation provides the communal support for such a vocation. Such accomplishment is unspectacular and very unrevolutionary, but it is enough to forbid the assumption that *only* in radical new forms can the Church perform a witness." [5]

Although the content of this book centers on the "being in the world" or social engagement of the church (for reasons mentioned in the preface), we are insisting that the true mission of the church is in all of the functions of which we have been speaking. Of course, a suburban congregation may choose to specialize in one of these areas, recognizing the difficulty of concentrating on a broad spectrum of missional activity. Or, a nonresidential form of the church may choose one key area of concern as its reason for being. Deliberate specialization for the sake of depth or effectiveness, however, is quite another matter from the truncation of the church's true calling in order to preserve the status quo and thereby avoid risk, or to make the church into strictly a social action organization.

We are now standing at a point of demarcation in the book. Beginning here we will be traveling an increasingly selective route, moving from a fourfold missional design toward examination of the "fourth" function of action or social engagement (*diakonia*). The remainder of this chapter, then, is a bridge between Part I and Part II.

Doing Our Homework

As the theology of liberation is poured into the mold of a four-dimensional design, many questions need to be sorted out

[5] *Ibid.,* p. 170.

as carefully as possible. Before churchmen can arrive at valid answers, we need clarity concerning the most important questions to be asked. In the remainder of this chapter, we would like to indicate five questions which seem to demand attention on behalf of intelligent social engagement. These five are little more than illustrations of the kind of homework that needs to be engaged in by suburban churchmen. There are other questions which are equally important in relation to social action in suburban situations, but we have limited ourselves to these five.

1. *Is the social engagement of the suburban congregation in the suburbs or in the inner city?* In one sense the question itself is false because the entire metropolitan community is so bound up together as one organism that almost any kind of significant social engagement in one part of the community affects the whole. As we have suggested in Chapter 1, there is a herculean task for the suburban church in its own neighborhood. In many cases, the most relevant mission by a suburban congregation in behalf of the inner city is dealing with the attitudes of suburbanites which have nourished the root causes of our present condition.

Harvey Cox has asserted that persons trapped in the jaws of urban injustices want liberty and justice, not mere friendly relationships with their suburban "guards" who drop in for a friendly visit. In other words, the relationship of suburbanites with the black community has too often been a hindrance, rather than a cause of genuine social change. Keeping this in mind, we must also affirm the legitimacy of black-white personal relationships. The gospel is a word of reconciliation, reminding us that God's purpose is the uniting of all men in a common humanity. Yet this unity can only fully take place in a structure which permits all individuals and groups to enrich one another through their mutual gifts, and this means the existence of shared power as well as shared humanity.

More than a few unconcerned suburbanites have been turned on to a new way of thinking, being, and doing by first-hand confrontation with inner city residents. When the statistics of human misery and injustice take on a name and a personality in the form of a specific human being with whom you have a relationship, then liberation can begin to occur. As in any real relationship, you cannot tell who is giving and who is receiving because the two are diffused into both parties. Both are giving and receiving, and both are experiencing liberation individually and socially. For example, a man who had recently become friends with some black citizens in a co-operative Block Partnership effort, bridging white and black communities, told us, "A year ago I was one who advocated 'shipping 'em back to Africa.' My concerns were only for myself, my family, and our well-being. Through these personal contacts my priorities are changing, although many of my friends seem unable to understand the change that I'm experiencing."

Concerned whites can work with inner city residents in community representation before city hall. The realization at city hall that affluent and knowledgeable whites consider inner city problems to be their own problems can sometimes have an efficacious result. As important as personal friendships between white and black people may be, these personal bonds must not be a substitute for political, economic, and educational progress for minority groups. The concerned suburbanite can personally support black art festivals in the inner city, thereby enriching himself and his children as well as showing forth a sign of goodwill. The suburban church can provide an arena for black artists and black points of view. By adoption of Project Equality, churches can wield some corporate power, encouraging their suppliers to become "equal opportunity employers."

The hope of the Christian is for a society in which there is an equitable distribution of power (justice) and in which men enrich each other through mutual exchange of their personal humanness (love). However, if we have to choose between (a) two more or less separate societies, black and white, in which there is just dissemination of economic, political, and other forms of power, and (b) a society in which there are frequent exchanges between the races and yet a continued overbalance of white power—then we'd better be clear that (a) is our choice. If we don't see this, we haven't heard a thing that black power is saying, nor have we heard the gospel's insistence that any apparent peace or harmony not based on justice is a counterfeit situation.

Whether a congregation centers its prime attention on suburban problems or develops direct rapport with inner city problems can be determined by an evaluation of the congregation and the inclinations of its members. For practical purposes, a congregation needs to make some specific choices as to deployment of its manpower in social engagement. Although these priorities must be settled in order to get off dead center, an approximation of a "both/and" response rather than "either/or" may be the soundest conclusion for many congregations asking, "Is our community action properly in suburbia or in the inner city?"

2. *Should we conceive our mission in the community in terms of issues or in terms of parish geography?* The former category is the broader of the two, presupposing the selection of certain tasks which bear on the entire metro community. Examples are community-police relations, citywide zoning

laws, school board policies, development of a human relations council, and fair housing. The category of geography, on the other hand, works out of a parish boundary concept, asking the question of problems, goals, and strategy within a limited area of the residential complex.

Some issues arise on the scene and cannot be ignored by concerned churchmen. For example, in August, 1969, the state of Texas asked its citizens to vote on nine amendments to the state constitution. One of these proposed the raising of the state welfare ceiling by $20 million. It was obvious to all informed citizens that disaster for thousands of welfare recipients would result if the amendment failed. In the previous November the same issue was defeated by the electorate, although prior to the election there was almost no education of the public. A mass effort of communication and support by thousands of citizens throughout the state resulted in the passage of the amendment on the second try. Many churchmen shared in the promotion of a favorable vote on this crucial public issue, regarded as an absolute minimum within an archaic welfare system.

Issues may involve churchmen in depth study, the formation of coalitions with any allies who are available, and probably conflict within the congregation and the wider community. As Lyle Schaller and others have pointed out, churchmen are seldom worldly wise in matters of community organization and use of raw power necessary for dealing with complex community issues.[6] We need to recognize this truth, and at the same time affirm the potential of dedicated small groups who work for changes on various issues. These

[6] For a penetrating analysis of the church and community power, see Schaller's *Community Organization: Conflict and Reconciliation* (Nashville: Abingdon Press, 1966).

groups can reveal the facts on an issue, arouse public concern, and prod those in positions of power.

Mission in terms of parish geography can result in focusing on certain social issues within the parish, and also on person-centered ministries. Examples of the latter are suburban counseling centers, ministry to certain groups such as aged citizens, emotionally disturbed children, or single parents. Frequently, as we shall suggest in Chapter 7, ecumenical efforts can prove fruitful in wrestling with public issues and in person-centered ministries as well.

3. *Should the church equip and enable people to live where they already are? Or is the role of the church to form action cadres for special missional assignments?* Both are legitimate concerns, and there is no need for them to be in competition with each other. On the one hand, the church should be concerned about the daily struggle of people where they are already attempting to be themselves, as well as mission to others. Where they already are sorts out into two major areas: job and family.

If we are going to be realists in the matter of suburban mission, we can save ourselves a good deal of mythmaking by accepting the fact that a fairly small percentage of suburban church members are going to become involved in disciplined missional cadres. Almost the only approach for accomplishing a high percentage of action-oriented cadres in the congregation is to establish a covenant from the beginning, in which cadremanship is understood to be part of the obligation of membership.

Most suburban churchmen experience their agonizing, hoping, hurting, and fulfilling within the sphere of their own jobs and families. If the message of liberation does not penetrate these areas, then the church is going to be basically ineffectual as a sustainer and enabler of human beings in the most significant functions of their lives. Through the mission of worship, education, and community, the church calls for a revolution in consciousness and being. This revolution of self-understanding is the basic task of the church, the hub around which the spokes of community action must revolve.

In our insistence on the need for a prophetic social action church, we can sometimes forget that our comprehensive task is both personal and social. As a matter of fact, most of the "action" that we deal with most directly as pastors tends to be in the former category. We are in touch frequently with people who experience various forms of tragedy or grief. We are called by a family who has lost a loved one. A man in the congregation has been squeezed out of his job by a corporate merger. A little girl is going to have open heart surgery. A couple is about to separate and they are wondering if there is any possibility of saving their marriage. A son has been killed in action. A son is facing federal prison for what the state calls civil disobedience, although he calls it religious obedience. All the lonely people. Unbearable sorrow.

It is our conviction that if a man is interested in investing his life only in social change, and is not particularly interested in personal ministry and care (insofar as they can actually be separated), then the local pastorate is not the place where he should be functioning, at least as a clergyman. Actually, widespread personal stability in the sense of authentic personal identity is a facilitator of humane social change and a protection against demonic forms of social revolution. Social change, as the fathers of the social gospel came to realize, can also escalate personal human dignity and freedom and reduce the debilitating effects of a warped social environment.

Before proceeding we might indicate several models

designed to equip people for greater insight and fulfillment in their jobs and families. Their inclusion is merely to be suggestive or provocative. For example, Northaven United Methodist Church recently instigated a "Dialogue for Businessmen in a Revolutionary Age." It was conceived from the Executive Seminars of the Aspen Institute for Humanistic Studies in which business leaders from all over the country come together for in-residence seminars in Aspen, Colorado. These seminars provide opportunities for discussion of the self-understanding and responsibilities of businessmen today. Two of the favorite quotes used by the Institute for the seminars are as follows:

> Men are men before they are lawyers and physicians or manufacturers, and if you make them capable and sensible men, they will make themselves capable lawyers and physicians. (From *Great Ideas of Western Man*, John Stuart Mill)

The second quote is:

> We must not fall into the fallacy of thinking of the business world in abstraction from the rest of the community. The behavior of the community is largely dominated by the business mind. A great society is a society in which its men of business think greatly of their functions. Low thoughts mean low behavior, and after a brief orgy of exploitation, low behavior means a descending standard of life. (From *Adventures of Ideas*, Alfred North Whitehead)

The first businessmen's dialogue was held in the spring of 1968, with Robert Craig of Aspen, Colorado, as the moderator.[7] The seminar was held over a forty-four hour weekend, and revolved around four main sessions in which the topics were, "Who Is a Businessman?" "The Businessman as an Individual," "The Businessman as Citizen and Neighbor," and "The Future of the Businessman." The seminar was outlined as follows in the descriptive brochure.

A dialogue for members of the broadly defined business, financial, and professional community, who are disturbed that the vocational aspect of many men's lives has become just a burdensome, unexciting, and largely irrelevant interruption between rest and recreation, out of contact with crucial and vital issues of the day, and yet somehow controlled by them, and swept along with them. The dialogue will consider whether it is possible for a middle-class businessman to find for himself both an authentic sense of integrity and self-worth, and at the same time play a realistic and meaningful role in the on-goingness of 20th century society.

In the belief that there is frequently a communication gap between husband and wife concerning the function of today's businessman, the seminar invited wives to share as full participants with their husbands, where possible. The term "businessman" was broadly defined so that a variety of professions were included. Although the initial seminar was composed mostly of Northaven members, we see the future possibility of branching beyond Northaven so that other churchmen, community leaders, and a mixture of racial backgrounds can be represented in the seminar.

The seminar functions in the conference style of facing one

[7] Mr. Craig was formerly associated in a leadership capacity with the Aspen Institute. Out of his many years of experience in the executive seminars of the Institute, he was able to bring a well-developed "in-put" for our first seminar. He is presently head of Robert Craig and Associates, Cultural and Leisure Planners, Aspen, Colorado.

another around the table. The moderator and the resource persons help to initiate the session discussion, which freely develops out of the insights and concerns of the participants.

For preparation the participants in the businessmen's dialogues were asked to read *The Dynamics of Change,* a remarkable overview of cultural changes authored by Don Fabun of the Kaiser Aluminum and Chemical Corporation (1967). The reader can imagine for himself an assortment of variations on the Northaven model, involving local persons as moderators or resource persons and a variety of reading material for preparation. In our judgment, the retreat setting is indispensable.

The next seminar may be centered around the topic "The Businessman and Urban Responsibility." Obviously, these seminars constitute only one weekend and involve twenty-five to thirty people. But it is one specific instance of the church providing an opportunity for business and professional men to be more significantly equipped for the task of being men in the context of being lawyers or manufacturers.[8]

There is probably more being accomplished by suburban churches today in relation to family life planning than in connection with programming for vocational renewal. Many churches are sponsoring retreats, conferences, and small groups in which various dimensions of family life are studied, discussed, and role-played. Frequently, professional assistance is used in the roles of lecturer or discussion leader. Professional leadership may include persons from the disciplines of psychiatry, psychology, marriage counseling, and psychiatric social work. The subject matter will vary widely. Exam-

[8] Another example of the church's attempt to engage business and professional men in discussion of vocational ambiguities and opportunities is the Yokefellow Institute at Richmond, Indiana.

ples are: The Emerging Family Today—Styles and Shapes of the New Family; Roles of Husbands and Wives; The Family as Mission; Love and Intimacy in Today's Marriage; Adults and Adolescents.

A four-session evening series at Northaven is offered by the church, using the leadership of Dr. Robert Beavers, a Northaven member who is a practicing psychiatrist and staff member of the Southwestern Medical School. Called a Family Life Series, the sessions center on parent-child relationships through informal lecture and discussion. A psychiatric social worker attends the four sessions and follows up by being available to work with a small group exploring the issues in greater detail. Like the businessmen's dialogue, the Family Life Series is offered on a fee basis.

Many suburban churches throughout the country have made valuable contributions toward nourishing a stable and viable family life by using their own clergy and lay resources, as well as assistance from professionals in the community. If there is any function which seems especially indigenous to the residential parish, it would seem to be that of shepherding and sustaining healthy patterns of family relationships.

Although the responsibility of the church to strengthen persons for humanness in their work and family living is an essential missional challenge, there are persons in almost every congregation who are willing to serve in action groups in the interest of solving specific community problems. There are many tasks which can be attacked more effectively with a disciplined and intentional group than by isolated individuals. If the congregation is working from any kind of comprehensive model, it will require a careful definition of which problems need to be dealt with and the recruitment of task groups to be the moving force.

Small groups of militant Christians need no apologies for their existence. The New Testament, as well as Christian history, is not lacking in examples. A more complete discussion of task groups and corporate and individual action will be the subject of Chapters 5 and 6. It is sufficient here to say that the church as militant shepherd will see itself as an agent of both personal concern and social change..

4. *Do we conceive our mission to individuals or to society?* The debate between conservative evangelicals and liberal churchmen has been healthy in some ways for both. The former have developed a stronger social conscience to some degree, and the latter have been reminded that the gospel is personal as well as political. Too often we have been asked to accept an either/or proposition. Either the church bears the word to individuals who in turn bear witness to the liberating mission of God in the world, or the church is seen almost solely in terms of political activity, i.e., marches, demonstrations, lobbies, or other action-oriented movements designed to change the basic priorities of society. The either/or is a false choice. The requirements of the gospel to care for the whole man, as individual and as society, should elicit from us a both/and response.

Virtually all denominational leaders recognize the imperative of the church to be ministering both to individuals and to society. A composite creed for the church's work would include beliefs like these: Christian redemption does not separate a man's soul or being or life from his physical and social needs; since sin is both personal and social in its origins and consequences, liberation is meant for both individual and society; concern for individuals leads to concern for the kind of social environment in which persons develop; no part of life, such as economics or politics, can be separated from

God's love for man or man's love for God; through economics and politics we can express love in the form of justice to the millions of neighbors with whom we have never had personal encounter; as the interdependence of man increases in our technological and urban civilization, the urgency of mitigating the social sources of misery becomes more essential; if we proclaim the love of Christ, yet take no realistic responsibility for unemployment, miserable living conditions, and exploitation of persons, then we are failing to see Christ in the need of our neighbor (Matthew 25).

The problem often comes on the level of the local church in the shape of a credibility gap. Again and again leaders of many congregations have vocalized their opposition to social action, symbolized most graphically perhaps in the hue and cry against the National Council of Churches, or against denominational leadership. Sometimes their grievance is with the means of social engagement, and at other times with the ends themselves. The inability of many suburban churchmen to see beyond the rhetoric and tactics of the Black Manifesto is symptomatic of suburban nervousness in coming to grips with our society as it really is.

In spite of plenty of evidence of polarization and defensiveness on the part of suburban churchmen, we believe there are more clergymen and laymen now who are willing to plunge into the social whirlpools than in recent years. In every denomination a confluence involving a minority of "new breed" clergy, an expanding number of dedicated members committed to community responsibility, and a substantial number of socially conscious denominational staff personnel is resulting in greater potential for the church's ministry to society. Many structures operating on a metropolitan or regional basis, such as commissions or councils on religion and race, also represent a keener social conscience on the part of the church.

In all suburban congregations there is a continuing task of exploring the scope of the gospel and the corresponding mission of the church. In many cases serious involvement in the community will mean internal conflict and increasing tension within the congregation. If our missional thrust does not involve us in the crucial political and social issues of the world, then either we don't believe God is where the action is, or else we are unwilling to join him there. The symbol of the cross is our reminder that there is no liberation without conflict. The church which is unable to face conflict is a missionless body, because man's need for liberation presupposes crisis, change, and conflict. Conflict is part of the job description of what it means to be the Christian community.

We can recall during the Poor People's Campaign some rousing discussions on our own boards: How shall we support the Poor People's Campaign contingent coming through Dallas? Should we urge our members as individuals to contribute to the Poor People's Campaign through the Southern Christian Leadership Conference, and should the congregation itself support it financially? Can we endorse not only the ends but the means as well? The sharing of these issues and others like them at least means that the church is asking significant questions.

In some instances the most realistic goal related to a controversial social topic is the achievement of an honest give-and-take discussion in which human beings accept each other even though they cannot accept each other's viewpoints. In other cases, some concrete form of commitment will emerge. For a truly revelatory document dealing at greater length with change, crisis, and conflict in the local church, we urge our readers to avail themselves of Grace Ann Goodman's *Rocking the Ark*.[9] This case study of nine traditional churches in process of change is an invaluable resource for pastors, small groups, lay leadership, and pastoral-parish committees.

5. *Should the congregation propel its mission strictly through (rather than "to" as in question 4) individual witness, or should it act as a corporate entity in the name of Christ?* As previously suggested, task groups can be authorized by local church boards or commissions to carry out phases of the church's mission. In this way, groups within the congregation can function on behalf of the total body. Or the governing body of a local congregation may wish to speak for the congregation on matters that seem to have sufficient clarity from the standpoint of the New Testament or of that denomination's stated position.

For example, if a board speaks for the congregation in approving the budget, as has been the case for years in most congregations, that board ought to be able to approve a fair housing resolution in the same manner. If a governing body can make decisions on behalf of the congregation in matters of real estate, property, insurance, membership, etc., then it certainly ought to have authority to speak out on issues of welfare, justice, and upgrading living conditions of the powerless minorities.

As most of us recognize by now, our local church governing bodies have been acting in behalf of the congregation for years in matters of finance and property. You can claim that these are not controversial issues as are civil rights and poor

[9] Grace Ann Goodman, *Rocking the Ark* (New York: The Division of Evangelism, Board of National Missions, United Presbyterian Church, 1968).

people's campaigns, yet many of the most grueling arguments in churches do occur over use of money. In fact, there are probably more guidelines available in the realm of social issues, such as social creeds and denominational statements, than there are on how to allocate financial funds.

What is at stake is whether or not the church will take on a prophetic posture. Prophets have never found a way to be prophets without risk and without head-on collision with the vested interests of those who prefer a mute church. The body of Christ, including his suburban body, is not always faithfully operated by popular opinion, but by careful examination of issues, the correlation of these issues with the church's reason for being, and by courageous public stands on significant issues, both in word and in deed. If we believe in the priesthood of all believers, we should also believe in the prophethood of all believers. Therefore, the governing body of a local congregation should consider the prophetic potential of its own voice and actions.

Unfortunately this principle of the governing body sometimes works in reverse (forward and reverse are, of course, value judgments). By way of illustration, the first time that some of us can ever remember hearing a public word from a number of Dallas area Methodist governing boards in local congregations was following the Uniting Conference in Dallas during April-May, 1968. A chorus of voices was raised in dissent of the Uniting Conference's "approval" of civil disobedience in extreme situations. On this particular issue these church bodies were speaking, in most cases, for their congregations.

What we are really plugging for in our examination of these missional design questions is the encouragement of local churches to discuss these questions openly, air them out, and attempt to come to a conclusion. Our hats are off to those clergymen and laymen who have diligently worked together in order to make possible open lines of communication for their governing bodies, especially in situations where honest dialogue has not been practiced as a sign of the Christian community.

The problem of how or whether the congregation can act as the body of Christ instead of merely as individual members of that body is, of course, much more complicated than we have even begun to indicate here. The New Testament characteristically speaks of the church as a body, and our concern is for congregations to explore what this might mean in today's culture. To say the least, the question of functioning as Christ's body is a significant one for our homework. A more extensive analysis of this subject is the aim of Chapter 6.

In this section of the chapter we have attempted to indicate the kind of continuous homework necessary for responsible use of our manpower and resources in social engagement. Other questions which deserve attention are: Should we emphasize the creation of our own missional structures, or recruit for involvement in and through existing secular agencies? What community organization exists or else how could we become organizers? Should we participate in social engagement as a single congregation, in a denominational pattern, and/or in an ecumenical cluster?

The specific style and direction, of course, are the prerogative and responsibility of each congregation. Generally, we have expressed a preference for a "both/and" rather than the "either/or" approach to missional design. We proceed now to the implementation of the social engagement mission, beginning with suburban forms present and those which are now emerging.

PART II
mission implemented

4

the underground
aboveground

Bootleg liturgy across forbidden eucharistic lines . . .
amorphous gatherings of concerned people . . . no address,
telephone number, or bank account . . . maximum democ-
ratization . . . unity as the by-product of concern for justice
and truth . . . sharing the Christian life and forgetting about
getting approval for what can be better done without approval
. . . a true sense of belonging . . . deeply involved in the
peace and freedom movements . . . joining mankind in its
life.

These images of today's underground church have caught
the imagination of many churchmen who labor in the

aboveground church. Who among us has not been pricked by at least an occasional urge to join the ranks of the modern-day catacombists, especially when the suburban scene seems hostile and intransigent? The vitality and freewheeling spirit of the subterraneans are a constant corrective to the rigid liturgies, lack of life-giving relationships, burdensome organization, dinosaurian physical plants, and institutional narcissism which have too often constituted the pattern for suburban churches. The underground movement has within it the prophetic voice of the free spirit, the imprint of the early church's care for the dispossessed, and the priority of sacramental relationships over divisive theologies of the sacraments.

The central question dealt with in increasing numbers of books, sermons, lectures, films, and conferences concerning the church is this: Can the esprit de corps of the underground movement become a decisive style in the aboveground setting? Can suburban churches increasingly be freed for a climate of more compassionate relationships among members; for greater flexibility of decision and action; for identification with the peace and freedom movements which seem to understand the New Testament with a clarity exceeding that of the churches?

A slightly different way of posing the same question would be: Can the suburban or residential form of the church take shape around the needs of the world? Can this form of the church equip and enable members for their ministries in the world? Or is it all but axiomatic that the suburban residential form is an antique, and must be replaced by *ad hoc* undergrounders, or by nonresidential forms of the church, such as in industry, business, the arts, the campus, labor unions, shopping centers, mass media, politics, and recreation?

In our judgment, there are at least some tentative reasons why one might expect the suburban church, both in its present and future forms, to more closely approximate the underground spirit in the aboveground environment. In previous chapters we have been concerned with suburban potential, a partial theological grounding for revitalization of mission, and an analysis of the church's missional functions. At this point we are considering forms through which these functions can be implemented.

Christ's Suburban Body: Metamorphosis Toward Mission

Out of the many changes taking place in the church today, none is more important than the rebirth of concern for mission, and particularly mission in the sense of turning toward the world and being "for" the world. We may frequently not know how to go about the ministry of servanthood. We may not agree on the priorities and means of mission for the world. But at least there is growing realization and acceptance, even if presently it seems like mostly talk and too little action, that the church *is* mission.

Our tardiness and sluggishness, however, have resulted in a siphoning off of talented clergy and laity into underground circles and secular humanitarian agencies. It is surely a God-given sign that the plush success image of the suburban church has been severely tarnished by personnel defections, the sheer intensity of the world's needs, and even the diminution of worldly standards of churchly success.

Metamorphosis toward mission means that a process of dying is going on in some quarters of the suburban church, resulting in the birth of new vitality and effectiveness. Occasional signals from the scene of the suburban church look like this: Celebration and joy in worship. Scaling down of financial overload on behalf of mission. Encounter groups and more honest relationships. Eucharist in the living room. Suburban action centers. Involvement in the work of city councils and other community decision makers. Courses in black history and images. Task groups for depth in education, for turning out the vote, for dialogue between polarized elements of society. Agenda shaped around the contours of community need.

These signals from Christ's suburban body are spotty and sporadic, and of course represent a middle-class minority. But then, the underground churchmen are likewise a remnant within the larger society. The underground aboveground in suburbia attempts to minister in the arena encompassing many of the root problems of this nation, as suggested in Chapter 1. Yet the gift of the underground Christians, symbolized by the contributors to *The Underground Church*,[1] to the aboveground church is not merely a decision about whether we will cast our lot with the underground or with the aboveground. The voices of the Boyds and Berrigans are also focusing on the faith question itself.

The Decision to Be the Church

Undoubtedly suburban church structures do need to be changed. They are not the viable facilitators of mission needed in our time. No one knows this better than two men who have accumulated twenty-five years between them in the suburban church. But there is a deeper truth which we conveniently hide from ourselves. This truth demands that we

---

[1] Malcolm Boyd, ed., *The Underground Church* (New York: Sheed & Ward, 1968).

look not only at the deficient structures, but at our deficient decision to be the church. In other words, the form of our faith may be more deformed than the forms of the present suburban church. For the mission decision is at least in part an internal decision as to who we will be in whatever circumstance we find ourselves. And if that decision made again and again is for a truly missional style, then that style will somehow pop out, poke out, and break out wherever these human beings are found.

Our oversized building payments do not automatically prevent us from a fair housing witness, unless we choose it to be so. The burdens of organizational detail are not insurmountable obstacles to identification with the oppressed, nor do these chores keep us from initiating militant social reforms or from the expression of pastoral care. The ultimate stumbling block is often our own lack of courage, our own faithlessness in marshalling the potential that in some degree is always in our midst, our own failure to trust the gospel as our final meaning and lifegiver.

The present forms of the church do constitute limitations upon us, just as there are limitations in all situations. We who choose to stay within the aboveground church should strive to change these forms for more suitable missional instruments, but at the same time be about our task of being the church within the limitations given. It is our task to probe the openings, and to maximize the potential in a given situation.

Are we saying that those who have abandoned the church in its existing forms have exhibited weakness or betrayal? By no means! The vocational question is a decision about where to put one's life so that that life can develop its potential of self-fulfillment and mission to others. In fact, we would suggest that those who have departed to greener pastures may have been more honest about the whole matter than those who stay within the present structure only to complain that they are helpless victims of external circumstances.

We will speak in a moment of emerging forms which would appear to enhance the missional operation, assuming the dedication to mission is present in those churchmen who inhabit those forms. First, however, a further word about the potential of mission where we are now.

The Residential Form of the Church

In our experience, the somewhat popular assumption that the residential form of congregation can be related to only one aspect of the world's existence, namely, residence, needs further clarification. The theory that the suburbanite "doesn't live where he lives" is well summed up by Colin Williams: "Since for so many of these people, many aspects of their life are not related to their place of residence, there is in the residence congregation this further restriction, that it is related to only a part of the lives of the members, as well as to only a small cross-section of society."[2]

The very nature of the gospel is that it can profoundly alter a man's root understanding of himself. Where this happens, there can be no geographical or functional restriction of its implications. A changing self will reflect the change in occupation, family, style of recreation, and in one's overall value system. As pastors, we have seen men make difficult ethical decisions concerning their daily work because of the influence of the gospel; we have seen Christian affirmation open husbands and wives to one another; and we have ourselves ex-

[2] Williams, *Where in the World?* (New York: National Council of Churches, 1963), p. 10.

perienced that once the gospel is truly "heard," life is never the same again. The late Truman Douglass spelled this out by saying, "I doubt whether the fragmentation of man's time and occupations, which is characteristic of modern life, actually results in a correspondingly radical dismemberment of his personal existence." [3]

There are today proliferating forms of the church nonresidential. These forms are indispensable to the church's task, and they include various mobile service groups, institutional chaplaincies and ministries, campus missions, night ministries, experimental ministries in the arts, industry, mass media, and leisure. Their existence points to the validity of Colin Williams' claim, namely, that even if the residential church does manage to profoundly influence the lives of some suburbanites, only a small cross section of society has been involved.

The church's nonresidential forms will not supplant the residential form, at least in the foreseeable future, but they will provide badly needed supplements. The parish church, with all of its hang-ups, is likely to continue as a base and foundation for the vast majority of Christians. In spite of dire predictions about the future of the family in the United States, nine out of ten Americans are included in a functioning family unit, and even by 1980 the figure is expected to be seven out of eight.[4] Those who claim the family-oriented church is obsolete must deal with these figures, as well as the figures mentioned in Chapter 1 to the effect that the suburban population is expected to steadily increase.

Without the fiscal support of local churches, it is doubtful

---

[3] David F. Marshall, ed., *Creative Ministries* (Philadelphia: Pilgrim Press, 1968), p. 90.
[4] Schaller, *The Impact of the Future,* p. 54.

whether many of the specialized ministries beyond the residential sphere could expand or even exist. Although there are not a few suburban churchmen who resist the direction of some of our campus ministries, we are deceiving ourselves if we deny that these campus ministries are not largely dependent on the suburban dollar in terms of trained staff and other financial necessities.

The greatest threat to the future of the suburban parish is certainly not in nonresidential forms of the church, not in patterns of family life changes, nor in the separation of vocation from residence. The real threat has appeared in missional retardation and in outmoded forms within suburbia. In other words, the church has been hurting not so much from the fact of residential parishes, but in the deficiency of the faith and forms within those parishes.

As already suggested, here and there the suburban church is already in metamorphosis toward mission. The film "Four Cozy Walls," sponsored by five national boards and agencies of The United Methodist Church and depicting the life style of Casa View United Methodist Church, is a concrete example of the residential form which attempts to shape itself around the needs of both suburban and inner city areas. The true significance of the film is not so much in the uniqueness of the Casa View congregation, but in the fact that it is representative of an increasing number of relevant missional styles in the suburban church.

Working in Existing Suburban Forms

For social engagement to take shape, we need to become sociological theologians who have one eye on the intersections of the community and the other eye on the missional apparatus of the local congregation. We may become gurus on streamlining local church machinery for social involvement, but unless we are also knowledgeable about the community—its people and their problems—then we are all dressed up with nowhere to go. Likewise, we may be very familiar with what's happening in the community, but unless we are clear on our procedures for task bearing and gearing up for participation, it is unlikely there will be any penetration or influence by the church in the community.

Today's obstacle is usually the "how" question. How do we choose the arenas of our concern? How do we keep up with what's going on? How do we develop priorities for social action and actualize them? What procedures might prove to be effective in relating the gospel of liberation to the concrete problems of the area? As far as official restructuring is concerned, the three key vehicles within any united Methodist local congregation for social engagement are as follows:

1. There shall be a Local Church Council on Ministries which shall consider, initiate, develop and coordinate proposals for the church's strategy for mission.

2. The Commission on Social Concerns shall keep the Council on Ministries aware of the need for study and action in the areas of peace and world order, human relations, political and economic affairs, and health and general welfare. It shall recommend to the Council on Ministries study action projects in the field of social concerns.

3. Task groups may be formed by the Council on Ministries, its councils or commissions, for the purpose of accomplishing specific and particular goals of the church's mission to the world. They shall be disciplined to individual and corporate action and shall be amenable to the Council on Ministries and report to it.

The job of the local congregation, then, is to sculpt this kind of organizational raw material or its denominational equivalent into whatever shapes are possible and workable for that particular congregation. The questions in Chapter 3 are ones which need to be dealt with by the Commission on Social Concerns, or its equivalent in other communions. If churchmen responsibly hammer away on these questions and others like them, some priorities will begin to emerge for methods of mission, as well as for content. By this process some blueprints can be established representing an intentionality, until the model is altered according to need or workability.

The local congregation has been one of the few organizations or social units in our society which has seldom had a defined set of goals toward which to strive. Verification for this assertion is readily obtainable by polling a few churchmen at your first opportunity, either clergy or laymen, concerning the master plan for social involvement (instead of for brick and mortar) for the coming months.

For a United Methodist congregation the master model could be a set of written goals submitted by each work area commission to the Council on Ministries. Congregations in other traditions would have similar internal agencies. The approved plan becomes the comprehensive intentionality for "missionology" in that congregation until achieved or amended. To be sure, the rapidity of change in our society means that a good deal of our agenda will be spontaneous responding to this emergency or to that unexpected need. Even the model for the next year or half-year will undergo rapid and radical amendment. The delicate balance is between steering in an intentional predetermined direction and hanging loose for the inevitable unforeseen crises which are sure to make demands of us.

An example of planned goals for congregational mission in the community, in this case developed by a Council on Ministries for consideration by the Administrative Board, is as follows:

Need: Higher rate of employment among minority groups in our society.

Goal: Continuation of our active membership in and support of Project Equality as a way of alleviating discrimination against minority groups in employment. This would help make possible a sharing of power by all groups of persons in order that justice and ultimately reconciliation might be possible.

Need: For minimizing the rate of crime by relating in a meaningful way to young offenders.

Goal: Recruiting of at least fifteen additional members from our congregation to be trained as Volunteer Probation Counselors through the existing program in our city that has been patterned after the nationwide program Project Misdemeanant.

Need: For physical and social activities for mentally retarded young adults in our community.

Goal: To work with Nebraska Wesleyan University, the YWCA, and other institutions and groups in our community for the development of programs especially designed to meet the physical and social needs of the mentally retarded adults in our community.

Need: Lack of significant human relationships and models in the lives of many children from Huntington School.

Goal: To organize a Big Brother—Big Sister program in cooperation with the social worker at Huntington School and involving high school and college students from this congregation.

Goal: To maintain the Child Care Center for school-age children of working parents before and after school.

Need: For transportation for the mentally retarded girls at 2821 N. 50th and the residents of Lincoln Manor who are unable for physical or financial reasons to transport themselves.

Goal: To initiate a transportation pool in cooperation with other churches in the community to be in effect by January, 1970.

Need: Housing and nursing care facilities for elderly are not adequate in our community.

Goal: To encourage the development of more housing and nursing facilities and supportive services to meet the needs of the elderly in this community.

Need: To get members of this congregation to become directly involved in political action and service in public office.

Goal: To encourage members of our congregation to run for public office.

These goals or policy guidelines were developed in the First United Methodist Church, Lincoln, Nebraska, by task groups organized by the Council on Ministries. Once approved by the administrative board, new task groups have taken on the responsibility for implementation. The overall planning task was seen in the proposal to determine the needs of the community on a priority basis, the setting of realistic goals which are within reach at a particular time in the future, and the decision on means by which these goals can be reached and the implementation of these means into concrete action. Goals were also presented for worship, education, congregational care, and congregational outreach.

We know that in many, in fact, in most, congregations there will be a relatively small handful of people who are willing to do the homework necessary for responsible social involvement. These few familiar faces may do well to limit their objectives to a realistic framework so that certain tasks can be done and done well. Unless there are at least occasional specific accomplishments, even those few who are willing to work and risk and fail will become discouraged from missional endeavors. The discussion on task groups and styles of action in the next two chapters will offer further suggestions on working within our present suburban limitations.

We can and should acknowledge the limitations of the present forms of the suburban church. At the same time we should also acknowledge the always present possibilities for social engagement. Without a decisive commitment to mission, not even a perfect form of the church, whatever that might look like, could give birth to the functions that we say we want to carry out. There are, however, discernible forms of the suburban church which would enhance the missional potential. We turn now to a discussion of these possible future forms.

The High Cost of Misplaced Priorities

It seems clear to more and more churchmen that we have been involved in a suicidal course in the development of present suburban forms of the church. This assertion has been validated by our own experience in the suburban ministry, as well as by that of many other churchmen. In the summer of

1959, the St. Stephen Methodist Church in Mesquite was initiated. The beginning was a vacant lot and the appointment of the pastor. Mesquite is a satellite community on the east edge of Dallas. The church's building committee was composed of open-minded members who did a thoroughly responsible job of research and study.

The committee asked every conceivable question that a building committee could ask, except one. A course on the history and development of church architecture was developed for use in the adult classes. Charts and graphs of expected growth patterns, sociology of congregational style, and carefully detailed expected uses of the building were compiled. The theology of worship was explored again and again as questions were raised about the purpose of worship, the relation of preaching to the sacrament, and the function of the choir. The search for an architect was painstakingly undertaken. No preconceived notion as to what the building might look like was ever developed by the committee. The St. Stephen building committee was determined to let the architects be the artists and designers they were trained to be. Following many months of thorough reflection and discussion, the building committee placed a comprehensive report in the hands of every family of the congregation. Then followed more months of preparation and further research.

The result of this arduous care and planning was the first genuinely free-form church building in America. Its dramatic, poetic, curving style was unapproached in this country, although slightly reminiscent of Le Corbusier's Chapel in Ronchamp, France. The building was described in *motive* magazine, *The Christian Century, Together,* and a multitude of architectural journals. St. Stephen became the recipient of several architectural awards and honors. The building was a major tour attraction of the 1964 National Conference on Church Architecture held in Dallas.

The late Paul Tillich, after seeing and discussing the plans with some of us, made the following statement:

> Without the courage to trespass traditional bounds and the risk to fail, none of the great architectural creations of the past would have come into existence. The design for St. Stephen Methodist Church is such a courageous step in our time. Only by many such steps a style of church architecture will develop which is the honest expression of our own time, and therefore will remain significant for all future periods. The whole church should be grateful to congregations who have the courage to create the new and take upon themselves the risk implied in every creation.

One would think that the constant attention directed to the congregation for its architectural creativity would have resulted in an irreversible devotion to the process of erecting church buildings.

As time passed, the one question which had never occurred began to dawn. The question is a very simple one: *Should we build anything?* That is the first question which should be asked by a new suburban congregation today. In 1959-60 it never even occurred to us to ask that question. Today, only ten years later, the suburban situation requires new forms and different strategy.

We are entering an age when the investment of countless dollars in physical real estate constitutes an act of apostasy on the part of the church. From the very first the building enterprise focuses the attention of the congregation on its own needs rather than on the implementation of a reconciling and risk-taking adventure in loving the world and existing for its sake. How can we really expect the downtrodden of the world to believe that we deeply care about anything but ourselves when our energies and resources are consumed for suburban real estate?

Paul van Buren couched it in unforgettable words: "Is it right that the church should even own property, much less have it as tax exempt property, sponging off the world's generosity? Why should we spend such sums of money on ourselves, when the world is so full of starving and homeless people? Is this how Christ treated his body, wrapping it up in stained glass, multi-thousand dollar organs, and thick carpeting? Whose body do we think we are, anyway?" [5] From the outset the congregation is turned inward. Its planning, its financial resources, its psychic energy, and its number one goal in its early stages center around the building. Like a child, the personality of a congregation is shaped early in its life, and reversibility is indeed a major task.

The justification for the edifice concentration is that it will provide a home base from which a more outreaching mission can be developed. This is not entirely false, but unfortunately it is essentially false. For increasing numbers of congregations, the combination of building payments, insurance, utilities, and maintenance amounts to an albatross hanging from their necks for years to come. Instead of catapulting the congregation toward mission, the building is more likely to become an ever-present millstone weighing down the freedom and flexibility conducive to full missional strength.

One pastor reports that for the past fourteen years the direction, or should we say lack of direction, of his congregation has been largely influenced by the strangulating effect of the building amortization. Another clergyman claims that for

---

[5] From a mimeographed paper entitled "Excerpts from the New Biblical Theology in Parish Life."

thirty-one consecutive meetings, the main business item of his congregation's governing body was what to do about the leaky roof.

A few years ago representatives of a number of churches on the east side of Dallas met together during the Week of Prayer for Christian Unity. Instead of sharing a corporate worship celebration, we gathered as a small group to discuss our various missional movements in the community. Each church was represented by clergy and lay representatives, the latter being from the congregations' Commission on Social Concerns, or equivalent. The premise was that the deepest form of ecumenism would commit us to cooperation in the community in behalf of common missional tasks. The outcome was disturbing, although not completely unexpected. The mutual discovery was that social engagement had been relegated at best into the background, and at worst, virtually out of existence. Each congregation was so strapped by real estate commitments that mere survival had become the central concern. The future had been heavily mortgaged—literally, so that morale was sinking and mission was emasculated.

A short time later a survey was made of the situation of the nine congregations. Data from each were collected concerning their investment in properties and buildings. The nine churches included Methodist, Christian, Lutheran, Presbyterian, and Episcopalian, and all were within four miles of the St. Stephen location. The average distance from St. Stephen was less than 2.5 miles. The results were incredible: 46 acres of land and $940,000 invested in land and buildings by congregations and/or denominations. Total membership of these nine congregations was 1,935 (754 families). Keep in mind that these figures do not include costs of maintenance, debt service, insurance, and utilities. If we multiply $940,000 by 6 or 7 percent on a fifteen to twenty year basis, the figures are out of sight. Today, of course, the interest rates would be higher. Furthermore, as expected by some of us several years ago, the increase in membership of these churches would do well to keep pace with losses due to mobility and inertia. In fact, one of these congregations has already folded, and two others of the same denomination merged in 1969.

If these figures were a mere oddity in the church planning of one suburban area, they would not be particularly significant. Unfortunately, they are more representative than we would like to admit. In one small area of Los Angeles, for example, church planners and pastors were shocked to discover nine churches of five denominations, with buildings worth over $3 million, combined annual budgets of $300,000, serving 2,400 adults and 1,400 children, and nine ministers who were doing exactly the same functions.[6] Leaders of national boards of mission indicate that these examples are representative of many areas.

How can this prodigal use of the church dollar be called right, wise, or moral? Not only are the initial and long-range resources of the congregation poured down the property hole (as one churchman put it, "leaving the church hanging by its properties"), but also the availability of reconciling funds for the healing of abrasive urban problems is diminished. How can suburban Christians, professing to be a community of care which champions the causes of the disadvantaged, tie themselves to the stake of the debt trap? Who will believe

[6] Grace Ann Goodman, compiler, "New Forms for Ecumenical Cooperation for Mission in Metropolitan Areas." Rev. Summary, 1967 (Institute of Strategic Studies, Board of National Missions, United Presbyterian Church).

that our crosses are symbols of a self-sacrificing discipleship, instead of a mere style of liturgical decoration?

The change agents of history will not be those who build monuments to their own religiosity, when so many are struggling for human decency and dignity. The church forfeits its prophetic right to speak a word to the nation about inverted priorities by betrayal of its own priorities. We can hardly judge the nation for spending much more for military-related matters than for health, education, and poverty combined, when the church itself spends much more on brick and mortar than for human need.

Emerging Suburban Forms

At least four alternatives are available for achieving more functional suburban forms, which advance rather than impede the likelihood of vital social engagement. All of them constitute a relatively new approach for present suburban extension programs, and most of them have a number of variations according to specific circumstances.

The first alternative to our present suburban forms of the church is what we could call a quantitative reduction of the present system. No new form is actually introduced. Rather, the drawbacks of the existing plan are de-escalated. Here we are thinking of the purchase of fewer lots with no ultimate goal of a sanctuary in mind. Relatively inexpensive fellowship halls and educational space could be built. Church agencies, such as a District Committee on Church Building and Location, or its equivalent, would carefully regulate the amount of construction to be contracted.

Certain ratios between present income and building costs would be enforced so that no new congregation could let its pride or uninformed enthusiasm blind it to the future financial burdens of excessive fixed building payments. Although new church buildings for individual congregations will undoubtedly continue, it is the conviction of Dr. Edward S. Frey, a noted spokesman in the field of church architecture, that almost no one will be constructing single-use building spaces for individual congregations by the middle 70's.

In addition, the buildings to be constructed could be designed as multi-purpose facilities to be used by the surrounding community. The results obtained would be less money plunged into church property, combined with greater use by the total community. At the May, 1969, National Conference on Religious Architecture held in St. Louis, one of the significant themes was the increased development of "social space" by new congregations.

The most radical redirection in suburban form is the congregation functioning without the burden of a fixed permanent location of its own, or at least without the usual building and indebtedness. This second alternative would amount to a kind of underground aboveground, not only in spirit and intention, but in actual form or shape as well. Certainly there is a wealth of biblical evidence to support the concept of a pilgrim people on the move. The style of a mobile, flexible servant people shaping themselves from the beginning around the needs of the community, instead of around a piece of suburban real estate, is no oddity to biblically oriented ears. The concept may represent a head-on collision with today's suburban values, but who said the church exists in the first place to inculcate values and images of the surrounding culture?

One of the better-known examples of a suburban congregation that has functioned without its own building is the Presbyterian congregation in Burlington, Vermont, known as Christ Church Presbyterian. Almost from the beginning these people saw their reason for being in the struggles of the community. To them the church is clearly not a place, but a people. They have demonstrated that even when a congregation begins with acreage for building (a seven-acre site), they are under no mandate to use it for that purpose.[7]

With a membership of approximately three hundred, this congregation continues to prove that a building of its own is not necessary for the congregation's growth or for its work in the community. In fact, it seems much more free and flexible to meet the needs of both its own members and the needs of the community than most churches which have their own permanent facilities, thus disproving the claim that suburban churches must build their own buildings. Monthly worship (The Festival) is celebrated on the first Sunday of each month in the facilities now being used, and members are expected to implement their faith during the week in the structures of the city.

If we suburbanites are ingenious enough to purchase land, get a building erected, and take care of it with zealous care—and we are—then we are resourceful enough to uncover ways and means for worship and education by the gathered congregation without a multi-thousand-dollar edifice. A mixture of rented quarters and the house church concept offers adequate resources for those who seek a community of loving acceptance, of joy and celebration, of outreaching care for others.

The Lutheran Church in America is one of the pioneers in

---

[7] For an extensive presentation of this congregation's history and mission, see *The Church Creative*, Edward Clark, William Malcomson, and Warren Molton, eds. (Nashville: Abingdon Press, 1967), Chap. 13.

new forms of the residential congregation. Through the leadership of Dr. Donald Houser, Executive Secretary, Board of American Missions, a philosophy of servanthood priority is beginning to emerge in the establishment of new congregations. Here are some samples of his remarks made at a church Building Conference held in April, 1969, in Chicago, indicating directions in which to move:

Mission developers are being encouraged to find ways of ministering without pushing toward erecting a church building. One is experimenting with small groups meeting in various areas of the community and with people becoming involved in issues and program. Another is using a barn redecorated and furnished, and according to the group they will be satisfied with this for many years. . . .

Can we any longer justify the investing of hundreds of thousands of dollars in brick and mortar while millions of people live in poverty and need? Can we justify mortgaging the congregation's future so that it is a constant struggle to meet an amortization schedule with little left for program?

Some of the basic principles learned from this particular conference look like this:

Function precedes form; but vocation precedes function. This vocation must be discovered by each community of Christians for itself. The vocation must be determined before a building is even contemplated.

All possibilities for the rental of existing facilities should be explored before planning any church-owned building. Construction should be a last resort.

The phrase "re-ordering of priorities" can mean:

Vocation before function, function before form.

People before things.

Ingenuity before money.

Servanthood before empire.

Service before survival.
Mission before mansion.[8]

An illustration of these principles can be observed in the Community of Christ the Servant congregation, sponsored by the Lutheran Church in America and located in Lombard-Downers Grove, a suburb of Chicago. As a matter of fact, this experimental parish seems to point in a number of significant directions for Christ's suburban body in the 70's. Like the Presbyterians in Burlington, the congregation owns property but regards the decision as to how to use it, if at all, as a part of the experiment. Emphasizing a commitment to "people funds" instead of building funds, the congregation is temporarily housed in a renovated barn which is used as worship center, art gallery, and educational building.

Jack W. Lundin, pastor of the Community of Christ the Servant, defines his congregation as "a Lutheran experimental parish based on Jesus Christ, striving for a sense of community and bent toward servanthood." Appealing unabashedly to the contemporary man who is disenchanted with ecclesiastical status quo-ism and yet who loves the church, the congregation is involved in six basic areas of experimentation. We mention these briefly, not only because of their own intrinsic significance, but also because they illustrate the direction and creativity of a "no facility of its own" congregation which has experienced steady growth since its inception in July, 1968.

1. Family education—There is no typical Sunday school. Instead, the congregation has made adults responsible for Christian education in the home. Support biblically, theologically, and psychologically is given regularly to the

[8] From "Church Building Conference—Focus on the Seventies," a paper of the Lutheran Church in America provided by Dr. Donald L. Houser.

adult membership in order that they may become comfortably articulate concerning their trust in God and that they may have both a Christian mindset and life style that will reflect joy, celebration of life, and willingness to become a servant of Christ.

2. Family worship—Sunday morning is reserved for worship alone and it is family style. The celebration of Christian community and all of its forms is done once a month, sometimes centering on the community of marriage, sometimes on the community of the nation, sometimes the community of the neighborhood or other shapes which the God-given Christian community may take.

3. The children's program as an assist to parents—The community conducts Wednesday afternoon children's programs, with the hour being oriented toward the seeking of personal and corporate freedom on the part of children. Its use of sculpturing, painting, psychodrama, role play, interpretative dance, theater games, allows the child to see before him something of a Christian life style through others.

4. Teen program—The Imagi Theatre and coffee house has reached roughly four hundred unchurched teen-agers. Imagi allows for freedom and creativity and in the midst of such open-ended dialogue, a ministry is conducted.

5. Organization—There are no standard committees in the Community of Christ the Servant. Instead, those who have a membership covenant with the Community are asked to permeate the existing structure of society to affirm it where possible and to speak prophetically to it where one must. Also, as an organizational experiment, the Community of Christ the Servant releases all members on the first Sunday of Advent each year in order to make them free for meaningful recommitment. As a by-product, the Community has no lapsed roll.

6. Listening ministry—The Community emphasizes

"people funds" and because of this is temporarily housed in a renovated barn.[9]

A member of a Lutheran congregation in suburban Omaha, Nebraska, perhaps summed up the "people first" trend of her donomination's Board of Missions by commenting "the main philosophy is that of first determining where the church is going, setting our goals of servanthood accordingly, and then choosing the fitting facilities, whether they be a stable, a rented building, or a unit of our own."

The ecumenical or interfaith center is the third viable alternative for newly emerging suburban forms. It retains the idea of a visible, fixed base of operation, but incorporates a number of advantages ecumenically and economically. Instead of sprinkling the suburban landscape with a multitude of steeples advertising our obsession with property and our scandalous divisions, the center concept would immediately incorporate several built-in advantages.

This approach offers a visible ecumenical witness in the community, since at least two congregations would be sharing the same land, and possibly the same building. All kinds of possibilities for clerical and lay interchange would be a built-in feature; e.g., one youth director for both congregations, lay retreats exploring mutual ministries, and pooling of office space or equipment. Grass roots ecumenism would be an inevitable concomitant of this new suburban form.

In addition, there would be prodigious and immediate savings of the church dollar. In the nine-church survey in Dallas mentioned earlier, a savings of several hundred thousand dollars could have been accomplished in one small suburban area alone through prudent management of an ecumenical

[9] From literature provided by the Community of Christ the Servant.

vision. The obsolete methodology of our present church extension is made all the more obvious by comparison. The tragic waste of witness, mutual enrichment, and money is in itself a terrible judgment on the church.

It has been only very recently that church leaders have begun to consider the possibility of mutual land purchase and improvements. In these cases pastors and people alike would know from the outset of the ecumenical center form to be used. The two or more congregations would exist side by side, with all the risks and rewards implied in such a venture. Creative scheduling and a modicum of graciousness could insure an exciting environment in which to be.

An approximation of some dimensions of the ecumenical center concept has been a reality for Northaven United Methodist Church and the Temple Shalom Reform Jewish congregation since 1966. Although from the outset it has been the intention of the Temple to develop its own site in another section of North Dallas, the two congregations have shared the same facilities with great benefit to both in terms of clergy and lay interchange, joint programs, and mutual enrichment. Admittedly, this is not the same as two or more congregations beginning together on the same plot of ground. Nevertheless, this temporary interfaith relationship has provided an intriguing glimpse of the fantastic potential in the ecumenical center arrangement.

Increasing evidence is available that churchmen are thinking more and more in the direction of the ecumenical center idea. The United Presbyterian Church and the United Church of Christ have entered into many local agreements that neither will instigate new suburban churches without mutual consultation. Joint development and use of facilities is being practiced in retirement homes, recreation and retreat sites, and student centers on campuses. A plan now under way in a southwest area of Houston, Texas, calls for the joint purchase of a nineteen acre tract of land by some seven churches. All will begin together in a huge portable edifice and will proceed to develop multiple-use fellowship halls and office space.

In the spring of 1969, the Broadway United Church of Christ gave up its costly but deteriorating church building in Manhattan and began sharing the nearby facilities of St. Paul the Apostle Roman Catholic Church. Broadway's former facility will be torn down, leaving the valuable midtown site to a commercial developer on a long-term lease. Although this is not a suburban situation, it is one more visible sign which will speak, through shared facilities, louder in behalf of Christian unity than any statement of words could.

Another proposal for shared facilities which has drawn a considerable amount of interest is the Columbia, Maryland, design. In this new city between Baltimore and Washington, a 25,000-square-foot building was begun in the summer of 1969. Under one roof will be congregations of the Roman Catholic, Jewish, United Methodist, Presbyterian, Lutheran, Baptist, and Unitarian faiths. By sharing one physical plant an enormous amount of money will be saved for community needs, youth activities, and religious education. Each congregation will have its own clergy, conduct its own worship services, and carry on its own pastoral ministry. The structure, known as the "religious facilities center," will be constructed and maintained by a jointly owned nonprofit corporation. Through cooperative scheduling, the center is expected to be able to accommodate twenty or more services over a weekend in the four multi-use worship spaces.

In the 1969 "Guidelines for Local Interchurch Action"

adopted by the Consultation on Church Union in Atlanta, joint use of building facilities is one recommended method of local interchurch cooperation. The Guidelines claim that "increasingly congregations are giving attention to plans which include the leasing of facilities to one group or full joint ownership through various patterns of fiscal and legal arrangements which meet denominational requirements."

The Guidelines mention a new Episcopal church which is being established in a neighborhood where a recently organized United Presbyterian church is planning a first unit. The two congregations have decided to pool their resources and build one building on a single site. According to the Guidelines, "the building is planned to provide flexible program space for multiple uses and a worship area suitable for both congregations for their Sunday worship, using a staggered schedule of services. Title to the properties will be held jointly by the trustees of the presbytery and the diocese."

In Kansas City, Missouri, four communions are sharing one new building as a united ministry in an urban ghetto. This ecumenical breakthrough involving Episcopalians, Roman Catholics, the United Church of Christ, and United Presbyterians is mission in a high population density area to people of widely diverse convictions. Known as St. Mark's Church, this inner city ministry can also be seen as a futuristic prototype for suburban churches. The building was completed in 1968, with the four traditions holding separate sacramental services in the shared sanctuary. Teaching, social work, and other functions are shared in common.

A suburban trend in this direction is increasingly visible. In the Montbello area of suburban Denver, the United Church of Christ, The United Methodist Church, the United Presbyterian Church, and the Reformed Church in America have begun a united ministry with joint staff and facilities. This united parish of Montbello provides for a variety of points of view and experience in regard to worship and the sacraments. Each participating denomination has contributed to the financing of the ecumenical parish.

Just over a year old, the Montbello congregation expects to break ground on the first unit in the spring of 1970. In the meantime, the members are using a house plan for a congregational base. Response from the community has been excellent, and there were over one hundred members by September, 1969. The Montbello plan will also be initiated in at least two other suburban Denver areas by United Methodists, United Presbyterians, and the United Church of Christ.

In the early discussions related to the establishment of the united parish, the question was raised as to what the members would be called. Will they be known as Presbyterian, Methodist, Reformed, or United Church of Christ? Or would they adopt some name in common other than any of the denominational labels? A layman spoke up, saying, "Hell, call 'em Christians!" This very phrase is now incorporated into the membership agreement of the congregation.

Arrangements in the shared facility plan vary considerably from place to place. In some instances there is a tenant-landlord relationship. Other designs call for separate and autonomous bodies jointly owning and operating one building. In still other situations there is a united or ecumenical parish concept by which two or more congregations are officially recognized by the judicatories of the participating groups as a church related to both denominations.[10]

[10] For an indication of the problems involved in shared facilities, such as legal aspects, financing and apportionment of operating costs, method of review and of handling special problems, Lyle Schaller, *The Local Church Looks to the Future* (Nashville: Abingdon Press, 1968), pp. 118-19.

A "hybrid" plan is also being considered by church extension Boards of Mission. It constitutes a fourth alternative for future suburban forms. Its affinity to plans number one (smaller and fewer lots, scaling down of buildings) and number three (shared facility) is that it begins with possession of land. Its kinship with plan number two (flexibility, mobility, no building owned) is that no long-term indebtedness is incurred through a building program. Instead, the property is leased for commercial use, and in turn leases space within the commercial enterprise in which to carry on worship and other functions.

The Community of Christ the Servant, mentioned earlier in the chapter, has considered the idea of leasing its property to a motel with a lease-back arrangement. Possible advantages of this fourth idea include no long-term indebtedness, a built-in ministry in the midst of a commercial setting, adequate space through the lease-back arrangement, and perhaps income from the commercial use of the property.

To summarize: the future forms of the suburban or residential congregation must employ a methodology of church extension based on missional expansion rather than debt-bearing static locations which frequently sap the life-style of the mission. Extension of Christ's suburban body would mean a community of people *extending themselves* as a servant people. Failure to act decisively in the 70's in behalf of new forms will mean missed opportunities for ecumenical cooperation, prodigal use of the church dollar, wasted time and energy in fighting the wrong battles, and unnecessary pressure on the patience and morale of those suburban churchmen who passionately want the church to fulfill its calling as a mission-oriented community.

5

task groups:
vehicles of mission

A Methodist pastor wrote for advance information concerning the proposed organizational structure of the forthcoming United Methodist Church. From the bishop who headed the project came back the suggestion that if he were a local pastor he would simply set up the particular structures that were needed to get the job done.

The bishop's reply characterizes the understanding behind United Methodist organizational changes. Like many secular organizations and other denominations The United Methodist Church's new efforts are not intended to be concerned about new structures as such. Rather, the concern centers on a clear understanding of the church's mission, followed by the creating and utilizing of whatever structures and organizations seem appropriate.

A primary instrument suggested by United Methodists and one currently being employed widely inside and outside the church today is the task group. What a welcome approach this is to many who labored through years of "permanent" commissions and committees only.

Some, of course, had already combined the two approaches, and many will continue to employ task groups along with commission and committee structures. A commission on worship, for example, might be appointed for a year's period. All the concerns of worship in the local church would compose this commission's agenda. It would study corporately and initiate studies for the congregation, as well as function in many other ways. It would have continuing responsibilities. In addition to the commission, a task group could perform the necessary work required in bringing forth a report which would speak to, and possibly for, the congregation concerning death and the funeral service.

This group would be called into being solely for its task—that of producing a congregational statement and guide concerning death and funerals. It would have no other business and would remain in existence only as long as the job required. When its work was completed, its life would be over. The number of meetings and the days, weeks, or months (even years) of its being would be determined by one factor—the need to accomplish a specific task.

Many persons must have responded to the concept of church task groups by asking, "So what's new? All 'they' are saying is that you ask someone to do a job that needs to be done." This is basically true. Task groups are simply ways of utilizing and expanding a method that has always been used in the church.

We must admit that there is justification for the accusation by some that we have given a new name of "task group" or "task force" to what was called an *ad hoc* committee. But more needs to be said. We usually think of such committees as having been assigned study and investigative work primarily. Task groups usually include the work of *ad hoc* committees, but also understand themselves as having been given the mission of putting their findings into action.

Nobody need be concerned about the titles, of course. We are concerned with a group that will not get lost in organization. Call it whatever title is most usable, but the idea is to accomplish the goals which have been determined. These "how to" chapters approach task groups with a very wide understanding.

Post-World War II churches often measured the depth of Christian commitment by the number of evenings which a member spent at the church. Neglect of the family and other valid claims on one's time was considered the price that must be paid to "do the Lord's work." Fewer laymen are willing to give this amount of time to the church today. The process of secularization, mentioned in an earlier chapter, has helped change that.

A need for community not found elsewhere and other personal reasons still cause some to appreciate frequent meetings, but these persons are few. An overwhelming majority of members have greeted our own churches' suggestions for fewer meetings with marked enthusiasm. They have welcomed the switch that calls for specific meetings for specific missions.

Any pastor or layman can think of an almost unlimited

number of "good" items to be dealt with at regular monthly commission sessions. Suburbanites, however, are not very excited about spending cherished time with "good" subjects. Most have said "no" to one or more desirable ways of using the evening in order to be present for monthly meetings. Many fear that each trip away from home will strain family ties one more notch.

An additional problem is continuity. Some of the most interesting meetings are forgotten by the time the group reassembles at the next regularly stated time. Unless a staff person or unusually committed layman can keep the commission members informed and related during the intervening thirty days, members will have given little if any time to matters previously discussed. Some will deliberately fail to attend because of guilt in having procrastinated or having forgotten what it was they had agreed to do. Or others may bring this guilt with them and express it through forms of hostility.

Ways of overcoming these problems are obvious to many readers, and a great number are more or less helpful. But a task group simply does not have to fight most of these battles. When the possibility of accomplishing a particular result is in sight for a group, the willingness to invest time can be almost unbelievable. Members will meet several times in one week if it seems necessary and if their time will allow. They know that this is not an endless assignment. And it is they, the task group members, who have decided how often and how long they will meet.

Self-determination is vital throughout society in an increasing degree. Efforts of cities to go into slum areas and remodel them, "improve" them, and make other changes have often had poor results and even led to a worsening of the situation.

The problem has come from a failure to include the feelings and opinions of the residents in the planning. Community organization has been imperative to any efforts toward changes.

Whatever else has been involved in campus revolt, certainly the claim for inclusion of students in policy making has been included and is often at the very center. Surely this is even more obvious to many through our blunders in our work with blacks. Self-determination is the very key to much of the black man's need.

This is no less true in the church. A group which has voluntarily assumed a task and then determines its own method and schedule in going about it is motivationally miles ahead of the commission which ordinarily has so much of its life predetermined. We have found that attendance at task group sessions is usually taken far more seriously, and this often is quite indicative of the level of work that can be expected.

Flexibility of meeting places is another big plus for task groups. Their size and the nature of their work often bring about meetings in homes and "on location" of certain tasks. The members can make their own decision each time concerning the most desirable place for their following session.

Nonchurch members can be included in task groups easily. Like church members, these persons are far more likely to respond to invitations to participate in a highly defined task. Many communities have a number of specially qualified persons who are not willing to participate regularly in a church, but who will voluntarily contribute much to task groups at work in their special field of interest. An architect friend of ours, for example, has freely given an enormous number of hours in a community planning effort in the ghetto. The cost of such time would have been prohibitive to the churches and agencies involved.

This "new" plan also allows us to utilize our own resources better by enabling a person to contribute to more than one area during the course of a year. It is not unusual for the same person to be potentially one of the most capable leaders and participants in several areas. But past organizations often limited or greatly diminished the contributions of a very knowledgeable man in education because of his year-long assignment to the committee or commission on finance. Although we have the constant danger of a few people carrying most of the work and depriving others of developing leadership, careful oversight can minimize this problem.

The seemingly democratic gesture of attempting to recruit different persons for every task can result not only in half-accomplished mission, but can also be very frustrating to those who are inexperienced and lacking in knowledge of their assignment. The arbitrary limiting of the more capable leaders to one area often results in a decrease of participaton by others because of their frustration in poor organization and lack of direction.

Laymen or pastors who are "specialists" in worship, but know little about church finance or Christian social concerns, could well be the greatest hindrances to meaningful and significant worship. The same might be said by reversing the order or introducing other areas. The mission of the church is one. To fragment it not only ignores vital concerns but also perverts the fragments by robbing them of their wider church participation. Wide participation is vital.

Our congregations have often found that our most capable leaders have been the very persons who were most sensitive to the need of involving others and who were most skilled in accomplishing this. They are also the ones who often begin to move beyond the local congregations in terms of leadership contribution, offering help in the community and in broader church structures.

Task groups must be related to the overall direction of the church, of course. And they are accountable to the community which brings them into being. Although they generally run their own show, task groups come to life because the mission of the church requires expression in a definite area. The group acts on behalf of the total membership and its work is correlated with the work of other task groups, continuing commissions or committees, or the congregation. This is done through the Council on Ministries, the Administrative Board, or the Charge Conference in The United Methodist Church, all of which have their counterparts in other denominations.

Our congregations, like a number of congregations throughout the church, have come to understand worship as primary to their lives. Services of worship, basically on Sunday morning, are central. The liturgy not only reflects but contributes to the mission and to the understanding which a congregation has of itself. This awareness of the importance of common expression and proclamation has created a call for deeper understandings of all areas of our cultic acts. Thus task groups have been asked to create a "Wedding Report," a "Baptismal Report," and the "Funeral and Death Report" mentioned previously.

Examples of task groups in which much less theological study was necessary are plentiful, of course. Casa View congregation was able to provide more serviceable and helpful classroom space through planning and execution by an assigned group. The group studied their existing structure, considered the number and sizes of classes needing better facilities, and utilized professional estimates to determine what might be accomplished. Persons knowledgeable in Christian education as well as those acquainted with architecture and building procedures were included. Some were members and some were not. All participated in the physical labor.

Recently a task group took the responsibility of hosting a drama troup for a weekend. The students were from an out-of-town Catholic high school. Details required to accomplish the purpose were many and varied. Several subgroups came into being. These subgroups are important to most task groups. They center attention in even more precise areas, and then relate their work to the total work to be accomplished.

Task group efforts involving the wider community more directly can be illustrated through intense efforts of our congregations to bring a Human Relations Commission to our city. Another group joined with community persons in the ghetto to repair a community center. The request of a neighborhood church to help organize a weekday kindergarten in a disadvantaged area caused still another task group to be born.

In *Rocking the Ark,* also mentioned in Chapter 3, Grace Ann Goodman presents case studies of nine churches in their process of change. Present in many of these studies are references to task groups. Some of these groups had very definite and specific tasks, while others were very broad. Some required extensive study and theological grounding in order to function. But with their differences they were all based on a common idea—the creation of structure whose direction and length of existence was determined by the accomplishing of a task.

A Presbyterian pastor told us that he has moved to task

groups for one reason—he wants to get the work done and this is the only way that it really gets accomplished. He is willing to leave "housekeeping chores" to committees and commissions, but he believes that the thrust of the church must come through task groups. He has found new interest from people who had begun to refuse "regular" jobs, but who are now willing to take a task group assignment.

"Don't disturb the existing groups," says a pastor of a large and fashionable church of another denomination. "I let them think that they are still running things, but I create task groups when I want to see things happen."

Although we question how long this kind of arrangement can exist, we point to this last church as still more evidence of the widespread belief in the need for task groups.

Howard Moody, pastor of Judson Memorial Church in New York, was one of the first to convince us of the need for a task group-oriented approach when he was in Dallas in 1965. He was most certain that the use of an administrative board supplemented almost solely by task groups was by far the best plan he had found for doing the work of the church.

Priorities decided on by the congregation must determine which task groups are to be formed. A list of priorities makes possible that long-range planning which enables a congregation to look ahead. But often needs arise in the community without warning. In these cases, the pastor or someone on a multiple staff consults with certain laymen in creating whatever task group is needed. The balance is that of weighing the need for wide consultation along with an imperative to act in time. A similar balancing is required in obtaining personnel.

Wider participation and involvement of the membership

can come from task groups. New members do not have to be fitted into an existing commission, for new groups are constantly coming into existence. And members with specialized interests or talents and peculiar schedules can be given channels of service. It might be possible, for instance, for some to meet at noon on Wednesday who could never attend an evening or weekend meeting. A keen awareness of the availability and areas of concern of the membership is vital for the Nominations and Personnel Committee and others involved in helping put the task groups together. The balancing comes in the work of combining a number of important considerations.

The availability of a person and his interests must be viewed along with such factors as: (1) how much involvement the person already has in the church, (2) what this job will mean to him personally, (3) whether or not his personality and method of operating might be very workable in one situation but a real hindrance in this particular task, and (4) whether there is sufficient leadership and organizational ability included in order to accomplish the mission.

Issuing open invitations for "everyone interested" is an excellent way of approaching a task group formation. It not only illustrates that the work of the church is for everyone, not just a chosen few, but actually enlists people from time to time whose potential contribution to the mission of the church had been overlooked. Rarely is the open invitation nearly enough, however, for most of us. Personal or telephone contacts of specific individuals seem almost always necessary.

The preceding paragraphs have made evident the side benefits of working through task groups. The church that follows this procedure carefully will become more sensitive to its own membership. Needed contacts with the membership are not only much wider but also much deeper. And the relatively short life and new formation of the groups can enable persons to be related to a greater number of people in the context of serious work, not just social meeting.

Unexpected developments can and usually do come from task groups when they have completed their time. One group completed its liturgical study and report but followed through on one of the "spin-offs" of its assigned task by setting up an additional eight-week study on a topic secondary to the original assignment. Often a task group will discover additional and unrealized needs in its struggles, and will recommend that one or more new task groups be considered. Even if the new groups include some of the same personnel, a completely new beginning is of great value.

If a task group aborts, there is no need for embarrassment. Information may appear which indicates that the task is not what it appeared at first to be. Some other agency or organization might already be at work and further efforts would be duplicates and unnecessary. To look for overt success in each endeavor is not only unrealistic, but fails to consider the many benefits accompanying the willingness to act where needs are apparent.

Investigation, of course, is an essential prerequisite to the launching of any effort. If other churches are similarly concerned, or if concern could be generated, ecumenical efforts might be possible and are often of much greater impact. (In fact, the ecumenical approach may very well be a vital issue in the whole future of mission.) Or it might be possible to supplement the work of others which is already in the planning or execution stages.

Who would doubt that many problems can accompany the task group approach? It sometimes takes considerable work to be sure that the same persons don't always appear as members of each new group. And if we fool ourselves into believing that everyone can and will take part in the church's work, we are fighting a losing battle. Some have no intention of working. Others are so lacking in theological grounding that without the presence of informed members to offer perspective, a task group could be worse than nothing. High ideals and willingness to work are only a part of the equipment needed.

As in other areas of a church, a task group can be robbed of an important part of its life if it is dominated by the pastor. The pastor's role is often crucial in helping determine the need and the task, as well as the formation of the group. But except for occasional consultative functions, the pastor does well in most cases to leave the group to its own decisions. This lay leadership is important to the present task and vital to future efforts.

To speak of the pastor's role in relationship to task groups is also to say much about his total leadership role in the church. It seems appropriate at this point to make some observations about the role of the pastor in the churches with which this book is concerned.

Little time was required by the more sensitive clergy and laymen to realize that recent increased emphasis on participation, decision-making, and leadership on the part of the laity did not lighten the pastor's load. Before much writing had been published about the emerging awareness of the importance of the lay voice, cries from the parish signaled the increased demand such awareness was placing on clergymen.

A friend of ours began a suburban church several years before us. Long before it was the "in thing," this pastor made a decision that the new church to which he was being appointed would not be the pastor's church. It would belong to the laymen and he would not dominate it. He was very successful at keeping his vow, but he certainly did not anticipate the severe problems and damaging church fight that followed.

Instead of everyone having a voice in the direction and policies of the new church, two or three families stepped into the power vacuum which the pastor had created by his hands-off policy. These few people assumed the decision-making on behalf of the total membership. The average member of the congregation found himself with far less voice than he might have had even if the pastor had been quite dictatorial.

Although this pastor was not clear about a definite program, he saw that there must be other alternatives. A church did not have to choose between being run by a small group of people or an iron-handed pastor.

Many have discovered that the pastor must assume a very strong role if he is truly concerned about the total congregation. One of our church members has stated that she sees one of the pastor's roles as that of looking out for all the laity, insuring that the less vocal ones and those with less push will not be streamrollered by the more aggressive.

Seward Hiltner says that "there is only one alternative to having a general overseer or supervisor to any kind of local group, church or otherwise, provided there is to be some continuity and performance of functions. That is to have so many codes, rules, regulations, and rituals that everybody involved knows exactly what he is to do—and is of course, therefore, likely to do no more." [1]

Hiltner argues that the pastor usually needs to use more

[1] Hiltner, *Ferment in the Ministry* (Nashville: Abingdon Press, 1969), p. 44.

power, not less. But this power is not related to status. He says, "Some kind of power is needed if service is to be performed. This ought not to be 'power over,' in the sense of overriding anybody without consulting him seriously. But the retreat to 'just doing my job' violates the whole conception of ministry, from the first and the second centuries alike." [2]

Pastors can become very disappointed with laymen who do not follow through on their jobs. Laymen agree to assume responsibility that is usually very different from their daily routine at work and at home. The subject area is usually constantly in front of the pastor, for here is where he spends his "working day," but it has no reason to appear in the thinking of the layman until he is back at church or in the presence of the pastor. Awareness of this can help a pastor to provide the continuity without nagging and without usurping the layman's task.

The role of the general overseer calls for the pastor to contribute the background of information and training peculiarly his, as well as his constant association in the field. He must be an enabler without manipulating the laymen into the execution of the pastor's ideas and desires. Hiltner warns that "general overseers are likely to stress their status and power and diminish their functions as service." [3]

Function is a key word, of course, that guides the pastor. We view the pastor as one who has been given a particular function in the ministry, and any other distinction from the laity is a violation of our understanding of the gospel. A pastor's efforts to avoid the exercise of necessary power in his office because he wants to be "just like any other person,"

[2] *Ibid.,* p. 45.
[3] *Ibid.,* pp. 44-45.

usually indicate an unadmitted belief that he really is called to be a little closer to God.

Most suburban pastors have the awareness to see that the congregations they serve need not be limited in professional training to only those resources they possess. We have found great help through involving other pastors of our own and various denominations in task groups as well as formal study. A Lutheran clergyman did more for one of our liturgical task groups than we could have hoped for. He raised the kinds of questions that did not deal with the proposed answers our group had. The people could have dealt fairly well with this. His background enabled him to bring the group to question the entire framework or ground rules from which they were operating.

The greater the lay leadership, the more obvious is the need of every church to continually strengthen its educational efforts. When task group members are sensitive to their work, they recognize the desperate need for more and deeper education. Persons need not be told that they "really *ought* to study more." The pastor and layman who go after their jobs with seriousness receive all of the motivation for education one could have. The educational life of the church becomes one demanded by the membership to equip it for mission and for life.

Our age did not invent task groups. We have pointed out that some form of this approach is a part of all history. The particular manner in which we are making use of them today might be radically changed in the near future. But none of this is really important. The important concern is that the church be sure that its life is not shaped by the structures and forms it inherits. We are called to use task groups only to the extent that they function for us in accomplishing the work we see before us. The same is true, of course, of any form.

Many church professionals, as well as laymen inside and outside the church, have become encouraged with this willingness to put the instruments and implements of proclaiming the Good News in their proper perspective. Churches such as Judson Memorial in New York found some years back that the administrative and organizational style is a proclamation of the gospel that is often heard prior to and above verbal pronouncements. For here the church acts out and demonstrates its attitude toward risk and openness.

6
corporate and
individual action

The argument whether corporate action or individual action is "right" indicates our tendency to polarize, and is similar to the debate regarding high church and low church worship. Or, compare it with the basic question of mission: Should the church concern itself with its own membership or should it be involved in the world? In theology, it might come at us as, Is God changing or unchanging?

Each of these questions assumes that we must choose one side or the other for our final and total approach. This is not necessary. Nor is it necessary to say that the answer lies somewhere in the middle. There are sometimes third alternatives that offer a more authentic approach. This is true of corporate and individual action.

We might say first that all action of the Christian is corporate, whether it is done individually or with others. We are all part of the body of Christ. Our action cannot be separated from the life of that body. But we will use the term "corporate" here in a less basic sense by letting it point to those efforts which involve the congregation in some common action. "Corporate" will refer to those ministries which require plural decision-making and execution.

The church in mission will worry little about settling a debate over corporate and individual action. It will ask which claims of the world it is going to respond to. Then it will determine the degree to which it will need to move corporately and to what extent the individual members will give a cup of cold water, feed the hungry, and perform the other ministries. Our concern is that of accomplishing our purpose. How corporate we will be or how much we will act individually should be determined in each specific situation. What does the mission itself call for by its very nature? The answers are often quite different.

Has anyone ever questioned the need of Christians to act individually? Hardly. It is the corporate action that draws fire. If someone unrelated to the church were to hear some of the arguments which oppose corporate congregational action, he would never suspect that its life has always been that way. It was not until this acting as a body entered the realm of social concerns that the objections became so powerful.

Pastors are sometimes afraid to act or lead without total support from the congregation on issues concerning racial tensions or peace efforts. They fear the strong objections that are likely to come. The new church buildings which have been erected throughout the nation become a part of the community, and their design, good or bad, has its effect on the area in which they are located. Few would believe that every individual in a congregation was at one with the decisions about these buildings. But fair housing efforts, attempts to extend the free lunch programs, and other such endeavors are reacted to differently. Members are nervous about *any* dissent, regardless of the number in opposition.

We fail to realize that a church is always saying something to the area in which it is located. If boys and girls in a city are receiving a second-class education because of the color of their skin, and the church takes no action to remedy this situation, the community hears the corporate silence and hears it clearly. If a congregation refuses to register its protest to a school principal who uses his student body as a captive audience for John Birch Society presentations, its inaction has certainly communicated a position to the community. It has made a corporate response of handwashing.

A most serious sickness of the church is exposed through its worry over the response of certain relatively small factions. These groups have a very powerful grip on a sizable number of congregations. The church's inactivity in the face of injustice can well disappoint a large segment of members. But generally these are not the people who form groups to get a new pastor, write insulting anonymous letters, and cry loudly about foreign infiltration. The desire of these concerned people for action can be ignored, because they will suffer silently.

The forerunners of the objectors to social action, in many cases, were those biblical literalists who were able to intimidate many pastors, and to prevent the pastors' open and honest interpretation of the Scriptures. The more receptive, flexible, and intellectually honest members simply walked away in disappointed silence if their views were not represented. Not so with the minority, who called for action that was drastic and immediate. They have been able to control the churches to a tragic extent by their potential and sometimes actual destructiveness.

To the credit of congregations of many denominations, the members calling for theological honesty and, more to the point of this chapter, for social justice and reform are demanding to be heard. Their full strength is not really being felt, and we are not yet sure how many will continue to work in the pressure which is always present in the institutional church. But the church is becoming increasingly aware that the adamant champions of past forms and approaches will not be the only voices speaking.

Here our attention, obviously, is with corporate action in terms of a witness basically outside the church. Reasons for a corporate approach to accompany individual action center in the fact that: (1) a bigger impact can be made through a corporate endeavor, and (2) more persons in a congregation are likely to be involved in genuine action.

An example of corporate action indicating the above reasoning can be seen in a previously mentioned effort concerning the establishing of a city human relations commission. Task groups at work in this campaign came out of a commitment of the congregations to give their energies and resources toward achieving a commission. A variety of approaches was used.

The Casa View congregation started with the pastor and four laymen spending two lunch periods looking at the possibilities of tackling the job. The laymen then assumed leadership responsibility and moved through the Christian Social Concerns Commission, the Council on Ministries, the Administrative Board, and finally, so far as it was possible, progressed to involvement of the total congregation.

During this period of becoming informed, several community leaders were brought to the church to bolster the educational effort. What is a human relations commission? What cities have them? How have they functioned? What are the needs of our city that could be met by a commission? What are the dangers? Where is the opposition and what is its nature? What other alternatives are available? These are some of the questions which were considered prior to a decision to enter into this mission.

Some of the action taken came out of decisions made at a congregational meeting in which small groups considered every possible way of approaching the task. Nonchurch persons already at work on the job prior to the church's entrance were able to tell what had been done, where action might likely bring negative results, and the particular needs of the existing private committee of citizens. The congregation had to be careful not to duplicate the work of others, or to form any task groups to deal with realms in which other agencies would be entering.

Attempts were made to find a wide variety of channels through which members could work, individually and through task groups. Resolutions to the city council and attendance at council meetings, letters to each council member signed by the members of the Christian Social Concerns and Missions Commissions, statements by the Administrative Board, letters to the editors of the newspapers and other means to educate the community, contacts with individuals outside the churches who would be willing to contribute to the effort—these were some of the ways in which the congregations made the planning become a reality.

The participaton of the church as a whole not only gives a vast increase in the many ideas and approaches possible, but also multiplies the number of letters that can be written and provides a great number of additional hands and voices to work in various ways. It also speaks strongly to the community concerning the seriousness with which an issue is being taken.

Again, corporate action does not exclude individual action, but can help encourage it. One opponent of a church resolution asking the city for a biracial committee some years back defended his negative vote by asking of those favoring the resolution what they had first done personally. Personal action is important, but whether one has previously made his own witness or not is irrelevant to a decision to act as a congregation to get a needed job done.

We have been looking at action that has been taken deliberately in view of long-existing needs, action that involved months of "bringing into being." It has been the kind of planning and work which the Casa View congregation did in responding to a Methodist General Board of Missions' call to bring a refugee family to the United States from Indonesia. The wide scope of work involved the locating of a house, furnishing it, securing employment for the adults in the family, helping the children enter school and giving them tutoring, enabling them to establish church ties (they were Roman Catholic), relating them to medical and dental facilities, and meeting countless unexpected needs that arose. Some incidents arise, however, which require immediate action, and are not nearly as acceptable to the total congregation.

Casa View believed itself called to act in response to an incident in its local high school. The principal had brought before his student body and teachers an officer of the John Birch Society to present a filmstrip which the society was attempting to show widely. The presentation was given without any attempt to hear from those who would oppose John Birch Society views nor was there any indication that this was one view that was not held by all. The church combined efforts with other community individuals to get immediate action from the school board and administration officials. It also set up a community presentation in which the filmstrip in question was shown and to which a panel responded. Questions were asked for from those present.

Not only did such action deal with the immediate problem, but the community became more sensitive to such efforts and was able to prevent a similar presentation from occurring some months later. School officials have become more aware of these attempts to propagandize and have taken steps to minimize the possibility of such one-sided presentations recurring.

Extended corporate action is being considered by another church in still a different form. A community center of The United Methodist Church considers itself lacking in adequate support—partly financial, but much more than this. The center, which works almost completely with Negro residents, is considering the need of sponsorship by a congregation.

One congregation is giving serious consideration to a sponsorship plan which would avoid paternalism and encourage self-determination, but which would lend the kind of support the center is asking for. This could include the education of those outside the ghetto on the purpose and ministry of the center, representation of the center at various conferences and meetings, assistance in securing financial help and additional staff. More volunteers might be provided to meet the requests of the director and participants.

The very knowledge of such support from a local congregation for an extended period of time would appear to be a great morale factor for the personnel of the center. It could also offer the congregation greater possibilities of deeper and extended relationships with persons outside its own life.

Comments on the task groups in the preceding chapter pointed to the advantages of beginnings and ends to mission rather than seemingly endless job assignments. Some pastors have discovered in a most existential way that most work of the laity is best carried out at definite periods. Certainly there are exceptions, but asking people to write letters "sometime," call on someone "when it is convenient," "give some thought to the matter when you have time," and similar requests more often than not result in minimal accomplishment. They can also bring a great amount of frustration and even resentment.

A pastor is involved in matters of the local church each day, and they remain on his mind. But just as he tends to become less enthusiastic and less mindful of community or district responsibilities, so the layman, as stated earlier, is too much a part of many other matters of his vocation, family, and other demands to keep certain tasks in his thinking. One of the best solutions to this dilemma can be found in accomplishing as much work as possible at stated meetings. Here a group works until adjournment time and accepts whatever has or has not been achieved. If it needs to set another meeting, this is in order.

Reports to an annual meeting of the local church have been handled this way. Instead of struggling with the regular problem of urging all those reporting to get their reports finished prior to a particular deadline, everyone concerned with presentations agreed on a gathering time ahead of the conference. Here they brainstormed every area of the church's life, deciding which report should include each event of the past year and each projection for the year ahead. And each person began to write his report, leaving the meeting when he had completed it.

Letter writing is another illustration of this. The post office could hardly handle the mail if all the vows of "I'll write some one a letter about that" were fulfilled only half the time. Awareness of the tremendous influence of valid letters on television and radio stations, congressmen, and other public officials brings far more intent to write than it does the actual posting of letters. By allowing time for writing at meetings of certain groups in the church, the intentions become concrete.

An Administrative Board meeting can include a specified period of time to write. Folders containing names of government officials—federal, state, and local—as well as school board members, radio and television stations, publications, and the form of such correspondence can be distributed each time. They can also contain writing paper, a pen, and even samples of previously written letters. Although one or two persons might be responsible for suggested letters each time, various concerns can come from the group, and everyone is free to write anyone expressing his personal views.

These illustrations make it clear that there is no one definition for the term "corporate action." A church can make a corporate decision in any number of matters that will result in varying numbers of persons carrying out the decision. Seldom does any church find itself with only one task at hand, and so it sees members at work in one or more of the several directions it has chosen.

Some members seem to have minimal motivation unless some decision has been made by the congregation as a whole and they feel themselves to be a part of the total task and working at this task in the company of several other persons. Others work quite differently. One person volunteered her services to a local hospital and has worked there diligently each week for the past twelve years without any support from others. Many have considered themselves witnesses to the gospel through their many hours of work in political parties. A woman who works closely through the corporate life of the church also works "independently" with a group of disadvantaged Mexican-American girls most of each Saturday.

These persons, found in most churches, are not really working independently. As some of them are well aware, their work might be done in the absence of other members and carried out strictly according to their own planning and strategy, yet they consider themselves to be very much a part of the total effort of the church. Without restricting them or attempting to overly organize their efforts, there is merit in efforts to keep the total membership informed of what these persons are doing, and thereby pointing to the multitude of possibilities open to everyone who will involve himself in service.

Much has been said about the need of middle-class whites to stay out of the ghetto and let the black man determine his own future. As a correction to the errors of white paternalism and a projection of the "superior" one lowering himself to work with the "unfortunates," this word is well spoken. Some still have not heard it, of course, and continue to insult the

Negro by attempting to impose a middle-class heritage and value system on him.

Another serious error comes, however, in the belief that all suburbanites should stay in their own sector of town and work diligently for the concerns of ghetto dwellers and financially support their efforts without some contact with the persons about whom they are concerned. It is true that in most cases whites need to get out of the black ghetto, but few can get out since they have never been in. Not that one needs to repeat the errors of the past, but it is a rare individual who can appreciate the needs of others of whom he has no real knowledge.

Corporate action of the church is one way to help accomplish this. Congregations can often bridge the gap between persons of different races in a manner not available to individual contacts. A Presbyterian church in Dallas helped initiate a program called "Amigos," which enlisted several other churches as well as those outside the church. It functions strictly as a social contact, but the results are intended to go much further. Through a membership list which gives interests, hobbies, etc., families are encouraged to arrange their own evenings or weekends together. The results are aimed not only at the deepening of relationships of those taking part, but also at witnessing to the community that interracial social meetings are workable.

The church that is clear about its mission and committed to achieving it will not worry about finally deciding between corporate and individual ministry. It will realize that neat divisions are impossible, and that every act is in some way a corporate act. The church of Jesus Christ will let the need inform it of the appropriate strategy and tactics appropriate to each situation.

7

missional ecumenism

The explosion of ecumenism less than a decade ago resulted from: (a) the church's diminishing influence in a post-Christian age, (b) the absence of previous historical reasons for separation, (c) the worldwide influence of Vatican Council II, (d) increased Protestant awareness of biblical emphasis on the oneness of Christ's church. For all involved it is an adventure into the unknown, presupposing a unity, and perhaps a union, to be discovered as we converge (not convert) into some yet undetermined shape or form.

The initial excitement of the ecumenical movement, however, has now given way to a more sober mood. The novelty is gone and so are the easy expectations that may have existed for some churchmen. Perhaps the prevailing situation in ecumenical circles is similar to the experience of the civil rights movement. Both these endeavors attained a fever pitch enthusiasm several years ago but have now been replaced with a more agonizing appraisal of the realities involved. Furthermore, more and more churchmen are asking if the price of unity is a barrier or an impetus to mission.

Intramural Ecumenism

In the early 60's the "getting-to-know-you" stage of ecumenism was in process on the local level. The intention of this phase of ecumenism was to create a climate of dialogue instead of diatribe, to break down barriers and bring about a climate of confidence, to dispel prejudice and provide a taste of the universal church. Although churchmen believed that this early phase of grass roots ecumenism would have a bearing on the relationship of the church to the world, it actually was primarily an intramural movement, having to do with relationships among Christians rather than between the church and society. For many Christians, both Protestants and Roman Catholics, it was their first experience of the catholicity of the church, their first personal encounter with the richness and diversity within the Christian community, and their first real awareness of the scandal of competitive denominationalism.

For the most part, the coming together of separated brethren took place in two ways. One could be called celebrations, or symbolic events, which dramatized and symbolized the new vision of the church. Observances during the Week of Prayer for Christian Unity brought many Protestants and Roman Catholics together for the first time in public expression of their mutual recognition. Reformation services began to recognize the post–civil war mentality, and Roman Catholics were invited to share in the celebration of the new reformation involving the whole church.

The second method by which churchmen expressed their expanding consciousness was through small group encounters. Living room dialogues throughout the country have personalized the ecumenical movement for thousands of lay Christians. Protestant and Roman Catholic clergymen and laymen have shared retreats and studies together, thereby reinforcing one another in spite of their admitted differences.

A growing relationship between the St. Stephen United Methodist Church and the St. Pius X Roman Catholic Church of Dallas illustrates some of the dimensions of the new reformation possible in the early 60's. In December, 1962, St. Stephen dedicated its first building unit. Various Protestant clergymen in the neighborhood were invited to participate in the dedicatory worship services. At the suggestion of a layman on the Commission on Worship, an invitation was extended to St. Pius for a priest to be present at one of the services. The invitation was accepted, and one of the priests offered a prayer and brought greetings from his parish. Shortly thereafter, he came again to St. Stephen as a speaker on the Second Vatican Council, which was in progress at that time.

A short time later, St. Pius invited members of St. Stephen to be special guests at a demonstration Mass. For a number of our Methodist people, it was their first exposure to the Roman Catholic Mass. Soon thereafter, several from St. Stephen were guests at the Confraternity on Christian Doctrine held at St. Pius. The relationship between the two churches did not develop according to any predetermined blueprint, but seemed to be born in our mutual efforts toward understanding.

After the passage of several months, a family night to be

held at St. Stephen was planned. St. Stephen people prepared for this occasion through an adult class study of *An American Dialogue* by Robert McAfee Brown and the late Gustave Weigel. For many of the Roman Catholics it was their first time to be in a Protestant church building. Some fifty families from each congregation broke bread together in what for them was a time of genuine excitement. After dinner, the order of worship of the St. Stephen congregation was distributed and explained, providing something of an equivalent of the demonstration Mass provided for St. Stephen people several months earlier at St. Pius. Then a panel of two clergymen and two laymen discussed Protestant–Roman Catholic relations; questions from the floor followed.

That evening will not be forgotten by those who participated. It was clearly a breakthrough in human relationships and in an expanding Christian vision. In some cases members of St. Pius and St. Stephen who lived in the same block came together. In one family two brothers came together, one being a member of St. Pius and one of St. Stephen. Their churches were bringing them together into a wider community of brotherhood.

The next January the two congregations spearheaded the Week of Prayer for Christian Unity on the east side of Dallas County by securing Dr. Albert C. Outler from the Perkins School of Theology and Bishop Thomas Gorman of the Dallas–Forth Worth Diocese as speakers. The two men had recently spent time and energy at Vatican II and were in a strategic position to provide the leadership we sought. A local high school auditorium was rented for the occasion. The choir was composed of St. Pius and St. Stephen members. In planning the anthems, the St. Pius laymen suggested "A Mighty Fortress Is Our God." St. Stephen members countered with the suggestion "Adoramus Te," and these became the two anthems for the evening. A congregation of some five hundred Roman Catholics and Protestants prayed together and made an offering for the interfaith chapel which was to be constructed at the Terrell State Hospital in Terrell, Texas. Only five or six years ago these steps seemed quite momentous and were in fact a trailblazing relationship in the area.

One other cooperative effort between the two congregations deserves mention. On one or two occasions laymen from St. Pius and St. Stephen canvassed new suburban housing areas together. The purpose was to discover the church preferences of the new occupants and provide information about the nearest location of their preferences, whether Roman Catholic, Methodist, Baptist, Presbyterian, Lutheran, or whatever. An interesting phenomenon was reported by every team of canvassers. Either the neighborhood which they canvassed just happened to be the friendliest community they had ever experienced, or there was something about the presence of a Roman Catholic–Protestant combination that intrigued and opened up the suburbanites whose homes were surveyed. One can certainly question whether or not suburban canvassing is a worthwhile function to be performed. It may make sense if it is the bearer of the word that men can be reconciled and can work together in honest concern for other human beings.

Ecumenical Direction: For the Mission

In all of this we believe one compelling fact has now disclosed itself, and that is the necessity for ecumenism to stylize itself in a missional form. For Protestants in particular, concern with the effect of our dividedness and multiplicity originated as a missional concern. Whereas the scandal of separatism had become accepted or even favored in the West, in Africa and Asia it was seen by the young churches for what it is—an intolerable contradiction. The church discredited its own word when it proclaimed the message of unity and reconciliation, yet could not unify or reconcile itself.

So far, most ecumenism has been primarily inner-directed, that is, concerned with strengthening ties among churchmen. The time is overdue for our ecumenism on the suburban scene to become outer-directed and community-oriented. The ecumenical sounds of celebration must rejoice not only in a newfound discovery of our brothers in Christ but also in our intentions to discover together the world around us. Otherwise, our occasional symbolization of oneness during the Week of Prayer for Christian Unity, etc., will become little more than a game Christians play in order to cover up our competitiveness and dividedness during the rest of the year. Unless we find ways for working together in mission throughout the year, the Week of Prayer for Christian Unity may become a masquerade which protects us from being the body of Christ in the community. The decline of interest in ecumenism in some circles is due to the awareness that huddling together means little unless we gather together for mission.

It has been said that the reunion of the churches as they are could be a marriage of the senile, that ecumenism is merely the repackaging of a product for which there is an ever-shrinking market. Unless the ecumenical movement becomes a missional movement in more direct and intentional ways, ecumenism as we have known it in its early stages may add up to little more than fussing and fuming over internal church dynamics. The remainder of this chapter represents an attempt to think out loud about ecumenism as missionally oriented toward the community at large.

We do not say that the inner integrity of the church is unimportant or carries absolutely no weight beyond the church itself. In fact we can agree with those who insist that Christian social action without eucharistic communion is finally about as phony as communion without commitment to action. We do say that ecumenism without mission, regardless of its style of unity or union, is not terribly important to the world. The force of future ecumenism needs to be in the direction of commitment to humanity. For the sake of the mission, ecumenicity is a goal which needs to be pursued in the now of our suburban history. It is not enough to gather together in enclaves of churchmen once or twice a year. If we are wise and faithful we will explore every possibility for working together consistently in the civilizing process around us, combining our efforts to be agents of both personal and social change.

A microcosm of the typical church situation in suburbia looks like a well-devised plan for waste and ineffectiveness. Experts in management could hardly conceive a more self-defeating scheme. Not only is there unbelievable waste of financial resources (discussed in Chapter 4), but there is also the absence of intelligent planning for work in the parish. Insufficient research has been put together for the purpose of pooling resources, insights, and specific forms of social action. Parish strategy is retarded for several reasons.

First, many suburban congregations have been consumed with concerns about budget, property maintenance, and related internal affairs. Our point is not that these matters can go uncared for, but that they frequently have assumed the dominant role in the congregation's life. The reason the Black Manifesto stung the churches as it did was because it was directed at our indefensible priorities. Second, as some congregations do become change agents within the community, they are sometimes more interested in "looking good" than in overall parish mission. The other side of that coin is that some congregations have to go it alone in parish mission if all the others are too frozen to move on the key issues. As indicated in the concluding paragraphs of Chapter 3, this is one of the missional design questions which is in need of continual homework. Third, planning at the metropolitan or judicatory level which involves suburban congregations is just beginning to build up steam. We will consider this presently.

Some Probings in North Dallas

Ecumenical mission in suburbia can have its origin in several ways. For one community it may be a burning social issue around which concerned clergymen and laymen rally. If not issue-oriented to begin with, suburban coalition may evolve from the concern of one or more churchmen about the effectiveness of the church in the community. Sometimes a special occasion may be used to initiate common ministry.

In North Dallas, for example, the 1968 Week of Prayer for Christian Unity served as a convenient handle to call together area clergymen and lay chairmen of social action committees of eight or nine congregations, who met at Northaven United Methodist Church for dinner and discussion. Our purpose was to probe the possibilities of several North Dallas churches for taking responsibility for common parish work and planning.

As a result there evolved over a period of months the North Dallas Cooperative Ministry. Several congregations observed our efforts and joined us so that by mid-1968 the Cooperative Ministry included Disciples, Presbyterians, Congregationalists, Methodists, Southern Baptists, Episcopalians, a

Reform Jewish congregation, and representatives from Jesuit High School.

Our statement of purpose and organizational framework is as follows:

> The North Dallas Cooperative Ministry is a voluntary association of congregations located generally in the area bounded by the LBJ Freeway on the north, Northwest Highway on the south, Central Expressway on the east, and Midway Road on the west. The purpose of this association shall be to conceive and implement cooperative ministries as deemed desirable or feasible including worship, study, planning, and action. Our concern is to be directed at both the North Dallas area and the greater Dallas area.
>
> Representatives from the participating congregations shall be appointed by the governing board of each congregation. Each participating congregation shall be represented by a clergyman and two lay delegates. The association will usually meet monthly, although it may meet more or less often according to the discretion of its members. Officers, elected annually in January, shall include a chairman and a secretary, who may be either lay or clergy. Organizational structure will be kept flexible and will generally operate through task force groups and *ad hoc* committees. No congregation is bound by the agreement of the others to engage in any specific activity or venture. All projects, however, will be considered by the representatives of all. Participants in the Cooperative Ministry include Presbyterians, Disciples, Congregationalists, Episcopalians, Roman Catholics, Southern Baptist, Methodists, and Reform Judaism.

During the first year the North Dallas Cooperative Ministry was mainly a getting-acquainted process, an information clearing house, and an experimental laboratory in dialogue about mission. For the most part, we listened. We heard representatives from the YMCA Detached Worker program, the Block Partner program being initiated by the Greater Dallas Council of Churches, and the Amigos movement, by which people of racially different backgrounds are brought together in various types of encounter. The Cooperative Ministry through its congregational representatives disseminated information to its member churches and kept alive the possibility of a greater vision ahead.

One specific accomplishment during the first year of the Cooperative Ministry was financial support for two detached workers who spend several evenings each week in an inner city area of whites, blacks, and Mexican-Americans. Their function is to relate to youth on the streets, organize small groups which undertake constructive activities, and provide adult models which youth can trust and emulate. Over a period of years the YMCA Detached Worker program has proved to be an effective means of relating to youth who otherwise would have little hope of self-development or of making a contribution to society.

Toward the end of our initial year the Cooperative Ministry began to lay the groundwork for a more comprehensive missional model. A planning retreat was held in January, 1969, in which some forty representatives of the ten congregations assembled to consider an expanding future. Four main areas of concern were designed for presentation, to be followed by workshops and further discussion by the group as a whole. The four areas were: (1) Issue Forum, (2) Parish School of Theology and Culture, (3) Youth Ministry, (4) Task Groups. During the 1969 Week of Prayer for Christian Unity, representatives of the governing bodies of the Cooperative Ministry members met to hear a review of our first year and a preview of future goals.

Before going further let us make clear that we have no success story to offer. The participation by the various churches has been irregular, and after almost every meeting we wonder whether or not we are really going anywhere with the Cooperative Ministry. Already we have learned that whatever significance is forthcoming from the Cooperative Ministry will likely be in the form of small, dedicated task groups rather than in widespread participation. The tendency of too many authors has been to present their local church story as a marvelous success, saying little about the many disappointments and mistakes which inevitably are present in practically all our efforts. As a matter of fact, the majority of cooperative ministries have a life expectancy of less than five years. Very few celebrate a tenth birthday.

There are many obstacles to ecumenical mission, such as people's inclination to support their own congregation rather than ecumenical ventures; the problem of bridging the gap between conservatives and liberals in any coalition; the problem of pastors working together effectively and being mature enough for their laymen to be exposed to a more inclusive instrument of mission; the difficulty in educating people to the idea that we are striving toward a basic Christian mission together.

The Issue Forum is an attempt to raise significant questions before the community in order to enable a process of enlightenment to take place and to foster a concern among suburban people. Community tensions can be constructively dealt with through well-planned forums. Given the apathy and hectic schedules of many suburbanites today, we are under no illusions of being able to draw large crowds of North Dallas suburbanites, either churchmen or nonchurchmen. Even so, by pooling our efforts we can combine the best possible panel participants with the largest possible attendance. The issues for the forum are chosen by a committee of the Cooperative Ministry, and the forums themselves are rotated from church to church.

Our first forum was held in April, 1969, on the issue of "Life in the North Dallas Ghetto." A carefully selected panel which included an educator, a psychiatrist, a counselor, a sociologist, and a housing expert reflected on the culture and value system of North Dallas. Billed as an overview of North Dallas culture, the forum was attended by 150 North Dallas citizens who followed the panel presentation with lively discussion. Though our intention for this forum was an overview rather than an in-depth specialization, some clarity was gained on the source of some of our deepest problems.

The second forum was held the following month. Its agenda was "Housing in North Dallas." Representatives of the Greater Dallas Housing Opportunity Center presented a comprehensive picture of the needs and the problems. Future forums will possibly by advertised not only through church newsletters, but also by distribution of leaflets throughout the parish area. A leaflet bringing the news that Protestants, Catholics, and Jews are working together in the community should in itself be intriguing news on many front porches.

The Parish School of Theology and Culture or Parish Institute is projected as an effort to offer specialized courses and to train suburban churchmen for mission. Our present thinking is to assemble fifteen or twenty people committed to analysis of the community's problems and to promote solutions for selected areas. The parish school or institute concept is not a substitute for local church ministries of education, but instead a supplement which could make available some possibilities less likely to be achieved by a single congregation.

Leadership will be drawn from pastors, laymen, and specialists in the wider community whose expertise is needed.

An example of a specialized course which is needed in suburbia is one dealing with the life style of contemporary women. One research group at Northaven considered a wide range of tasks to be accomplished, and concluded that the lack of direction and use of potential by suburban women constituted a prime need for exploration. Consequently, a group of the women put together a curriculum dealing with broadening horizons of contemporary women, which was initially offered in the spring of 1969 to twenty-two women. From the pilot project we anticipate the possibility of the course being offered annually either at Northaven or in an ecumenical setting. An outline which suggests some features of the initial course and of the fall, 1969, course is as follows:

EXPLORE . . . A Course in
Broadening Horizons for Contemporary Woman

A kaleidoscope of demands bombards the kitchen door
Women are challenged to:
- *look* at themselves and the spectrum of roles they play
- *study* the changing needs of family, community, world
- *evaluate* the new possibilities and responsibilities thrust upon them
- *respond* with a life plan—each woman's unique way of saying "yes" to herself, her family, her community, and the wider world

My Self: New Perspectives		*My Life: Exploding Possibilities*
Education: Views on Learning	**EXPLORE**	*My Time: Decision of Commitment*
New Vocations, I: Volunteer "pro"		*New Vocations, II: Employment*

EXPLORE—a course of encounter via lectures, discussions, workshops, panels, speakers, reading assignments, art, music, and special aids to self-evaluation, including the Strong Vocational Interest Blank.

The teaching team of Northaven women will be led by Jean Swenson, formerly with the staff of the Office of Continuing Educaton for Women, George Washington University, Washington, D.C.

Time: Seven Wednesday mornings, 9:30-11:30 A.M.
March 19–April 30, 1969

Place: Northaven United Methodist Church

Tuition: $10, covers study materials, tests, child care

"Explore" makes use of intensive self-evaluation and time assignments; investigation of volunteer work, employment, and education; and a selection of readings (examples: *AAUW Journal,* May, 1966, "1982 Steps to Man"; *Great Expectations; Social Change and New Directions in Continuing Education for Women; Adult Leadership,* "Humanness and the Sexes" by Tucker, May, 1969; *motive,* "The Demise of the Dancing Dog" by Ozick, March-April, 1969.

A major idea which came from "Explore" was an information center designed to be an independent organization serving as a clearing house for women who seek to broaden their horizons in ways compatible with their family responsibilities. The center would:

Provide information about opportunities for women in the fields of employment, education, and volunteer service in the Dallas area.

Offer guidance to women who desire help in finding a satisfying expression of their time and talents in our society.

Sponsor programs that encourage women to develop self-directed life styles.

Encourage the development of more responsible, challenging opportunities for women in all fields.

Whether this idea will actually be implemented remains to be seen.

The Cooperative Ministry has been exploring the possibilities of ecumenical youth work. Youth ministry is by nature ecumenical in the sense that few senior highs have the hangups on denominational pride, theological rigor mortis, or restricted sacraments that many adults have known for years.

One of the most imaginative curricula for senior high youth is called The Academy, developed in 1968-69 by Ronald Devillier, associate pastor and youth minister of Northaven. It is the kind of ground that so badly needs to be covered with the youth of today and could be a prototype for a suburban parish institute.

The New World in Five Dimensions

I. *Theological Foundations*

Scope: Explore contemporary theology using as a text *God's Revolution and Man's Responsibility* by Harvey Cox

Content: January   5—God's Revolutionary World

January 12—Sin: Man's Betrayal of His Manhood

January 19—The Gospel: God's Word for His World

January 26—Sacrament: Suffering with God in His World

February 2—Ministry: Working with God in His World

II. *The Revolution: Political Dimensions*

Scope: To seek out some of the revolutionary edges of

our times which have political intentions.

Content: February 9—*Black Power.* Read chapter II of *Black Power* by Stokely Carmichael and Charles V. Hamilton, which spells out the intentions of this movement.

February 16—*Black Panther.* A movie and discussion of this facet of the Black movement.

February 23—*Chomsky-Resist.* A movie and discussion of the draft resistance movement plus an article by Edgar Friedenberg, "The Draft and the Generation Gap."

March 2—*End of a Revolution?* Film and discussion of Che Guevarra and the Bolivian revolution. Also complete diary of Che's guerrilla campaign in Bolivia.

March 9—*Danger on the Right.* Movie and discussion of various forms of extremism. Also, a special *motive* magazine article by Carey McWilliams: "Wallace—America's Self-fulfilling Prophecy."

III. *The Revolution: Scientific and Technological Dimensions*

Scope: An exploration of some of the scientific discoveries and technological advances which have, and will, profoundly affect not only the world we live in, but our view of this world.

Content: Will Man Direct His Own Evolution? Film— *The Mystery of Life,* an exploration of the present understanding of the mechanism of heredity. Reading—"The Age of Miracles" from *The Dynamics of Change.* Discussion of the possibility and implications of man's ability to alter his genetic makeup.

The Impact of Scientific and Technological Advancement: Films—NASA films of the Apollo 8 flight. Readings—excerpts from *Anti-ballistic Missile Systems* by Garwin Bethe and *The American Economy: The Many Failures of Success* by K. Boulding. Discussion of the varying ways in which science and technology affect us.

Science and the City: Films—*Cities in Crisis, What Is Happening?* and *Cities of the Future.* Reading—*Man and the Space Around Him* by C. A. Doxiadis. Discussion of the impact of science on the present and future form of the city.

Science and the World: Film—*Food or Famine,* a study of the problems and possibilities of feeding the people of the world. Reading—Excerpts from *Producing Food for the World.*

Science and Society: Film—*Science and Society, a Race Against Time;* scientists discuss the social problems created by technology. Readings—Excerpts from *The New Brahmins: Scientific Life in America* by S. Klaw and *The Common Sense of Science* by J. Bronowski.

IV. *The Revolution: Youth Dimensions*

Scope: An analysis of the youth revolution and the levels at which it is occurring.

Content: April 20—*The New Morality,* a movie and discussion of the new morality. Also, a reading from *It's Happening* by Simmons and Winograd, chapter II, "The Hang-Loose Ethic."

April 27—*The Berkeley Rebels,* a photographic essay on student rebellions and their causes. Also, an article on "Danny the Red" and the Paris revolt.

May 4—*Summerhill,* a movie exploring an experimental school for kids which puts preparation for life ahead of learning.

May 11—*Tom Hayden and S.D.S.*, an analysis of this political youth organization. Reading assignment—*The Port Huron Statement.*

May 18—*Families on Fire*, an objective look at the crisis of the twentieth century family.

V. *The Revolution: Art Dimensions*

Scope: An analysis of the revolutionary changes and an assessment of these changes in the arts.

Content: May 25—Music from Fats Domino to the Beatles.

June 1—Cinema from DeMille to Antonioni.

June 8—TV from Red Skelton to Laugh-In.

June 15—Literary Heroes: Huck Finn, Holden Caulfield and the anti-hero novels.

June 22—Magazines and the Underground Press Movement.

We are well aware that many suburban parents would have considerable hesitancy about this content, to say nothing of their pastors. Even so, here is an introduction to the world as it really is, the emerging world which the high school graduate will find on the college campus and on the world scene beyond the college campus. Here is an opportunity for wrestling with the revolutionary movements of our time with the guidance of concerned leaders of the Christian community. A Dallas psychiatrist who specializes in working with hospitalized adolescent patients has said that one of the most pressing needs of youth is the mental and emotional formation of sane models of dissent.

The pattern of family life and educational systems in most

suburban communities all too often leads to either a pattern of sterile conformity or else a dissent which becomes an emotional compulsion without critical reflection and understanding. The serious analysis and discussion of the world around us is unlikely to be offered to a high school youth in either his public educational experience or elsewhere unless the church picks up the responsibility. Many sessions of The Academy utilize films, and all sessions involve group discussion.

The curriculum is accented with the political left because the action today is from the left, from the revolutionaries who, for better or worse, are out to shape history. Any new world curriculum that is going to tell it the way it is will not be oblivious to this fact. If a congregation cannot at least have open and honest discussion about what's happening in the world, then there's little hope for the faithfulness of that congregation. If we expect our youth to take responsibility for the world, then we need to be about the task of responsibly acquainting them with what's going on in the world and its relation to the word which the Christian community exists to bear. However, our concern here is not to sell a certain curriculum, but to raise the question of whether or not the church has the courage to face the new day with its youth. As a matter of fact, the youth literature of several denominations, including United Methodist, has been moving in this direction for several years.

In addition to the issue forum, a parish institute, and youth ministry (some dimensions being in operation and others in the planning stage), the Cooperative Ministry sees the fostering of various task groups as a fourth main missional goal. At the present time the Fair Housing Task Group has begun. It will engineer education in the community, gather information on availability of housing and apartments in an area of North

Dallas, maintain communications with real estate agents, and escort potential Negro buyers in looking at available residences.

Other events or actions sponsored by the Cooperative Ministry have included a film forum; encouragement of its member congregations to petition the city council in support of a Block Partnership group seeking a humane arrangement with persons whose homes are to be replaced by expansion of Fair Park; and special programs and services during the Week of Prayer for Christian Unity and Holy Week.

The ecumenical coalition offers the advantage of comprehensive parish strategy, reduction of overlapping efforts, and a broader base of support. If members of an open housing task group represent eight congregations instead of one, they constitute a more formidable opponent for the foes of fair housing in that the malice must be directed at a whole group of congregations and pastors. Furthermore, the Co-operative Ministry approach offers a missional escalator for the progressive pastor who has just a handful of "radicals" in an otherwise conservative congregation. One pastor has remarked that the North Dallas Cooperative Ministry Fair Housing Task Force provides a mission opportunity that would be unthinkable within his own congregation.

Possible Prototypes for Missional Ecumenism in Suburbia: Ecumenical Centers and Forms of Interchurch Action

Although the suburban scene may still be dominated by an introverted congregational style of living in one's own minuscule denominational world, we are beginning to see an increase in suburban coalitions and centers throughout the nation. In Detroit a program of suburban action centers has been instigated as a white community organization to deal with the issue of racism. The idea of ecumenical action centers funded and staffed by white churchmen is gaining influence in many sectors. Suburban action centers have been at work in Philadelphia with the philosophy stated below:

> Since the Church's mission must focus upon the root causes of the problems of our society and not simply upon the symptoms, and since the root causes of the current urban crisis lie in the structures and attitudes controlled by the white community, we propose that our mission thrust be directed toward the bulk of our white constituents by the creation of suburban action centers. We suggest the creation of one center to be used as a pilot program.
>
> While we are agreed that the major hope for a new shape for our society may well lie within the initiative of the Black Community, it is politically realistic to seek to organize whites in such a way that the change envisioned by many of us shall be enabled.
>
> These suburban action centers shall seek to provide resources, technical skills and principles by which members of the indigenous suburban community can be organized so as to work for fundamental changes in the attitudes and structures of our society which will bring about genuine participatory democracy, human freedom and individual dignity for every man.[1]

Suburban action centers are likely to work at the task of bringing about changes in the structures and attitudes of the suburban community, and at the same time support the black community by such means as a resource pool available for

[1] From a mimeographed article entitled "Suburban Action Centers," The Office of Church and Community, Presbytery of Philadelphia.

technical assistance when called upon. Styles of operation include education and research, dialogues, confrontation, and political action. Concerns of action centers include housing, zoning, education, employment, creative opportunities for the aged, availability of counseling resources in the community, ministry to divorcees, group therapy, and organizing and sponsoring low-cost housing projects.

Organizational structure for suburban action centers may include a full-time staff member, an advisory board, seminary interns, and a suitable location for operation. Financial support may come from a variety of sources, including local church support, denominational support, contributions from allies of the center, and foundation grants.

Some centers, such as the Wilton Ecumenical Center in Fairfield County, Connecticut, have been functioning for a decade. Organized in 1960, this ecumenical center was located for a while in a small room in the village shopping center of Wilton, Connecticut. The center set out to be a concrete expression by Wilton's churchmen of their need to serve and care for the world around them. Congregational, Methodist, Episcopal, Quaker, and Presbyterian congregations have shared in the mission of the center. Like the North Dallas Cooperative Ministry, the first year of the Wilton Center is described by its participants as very tentative and exploratory. Experiments quickly brought two urgent needs into focus—two-way communication and reflection. All activities were shaped with these needs in mind.

One of the things tackled through the years has been sponsorship of public gatherings on subjects such as communication between liberals and conservatives, pros and cons of regional planning, and authority and freedom in the high school. The Wilton Center has also been involved in training laymen for engagement on suburban social issues, vocational groups discussing matters of mutual concern, a summer job registry designed to help youth find summer employment, and Roman Catholic–Protestant dialogue. About three years ago the center became a part of a regional ecumenical project working in eight communities of southwestern Fairfield County with plans for a paid director.

However, in the meantime the center vacated its shopping center location, continuing in homes and as a segment of the regional ecumenical project. Over a period of time the work of the center, especially its attempt to provide a ministry to youth, resulted in considerable alienation from the churches of the community. The polarization between the Wilton Ecumenical Center and the churches of Wilton raises a question which is becoming increasingly significant for the suburban church: *Will ecumenical mission on the local level constitute a vehicle for suburban churches, or will this style of mission be a detour around the opposition of these churches?*

There is uncomfortable evidence, both in Wilton and elsewhere, that ecumenical mission sometimes must be glued together and supported by a few social activists from several congregations, allied with like-minded nonchurchmen, but not really undergirded and sustained by the larger congregational bodies. In these situations the minority missioners have to make a choice between utilizing their rather *ad hoc* ecumenical group as an underground aboveground structure or else intentionally defecting from the existing institution and going it alone. Ecumenical centers, then, may become testing grounds for how serious local congregations are about their mission.

At any rate, some centers function through the efforts of a

few local clergymen and laymen while others are able to finance a full-time director. Other suburban cooperative efforts do not actually have centers and are more accurately described as ecumenical coalitions, clusters, or cooperative ministries. Since different communitites offer varying possibilities, the job of churchmen is to faithfully explore their own situation for the maximum missional yield.

At the April, 1969, meeting in Atlanta, the Consultation on Church Union (also mentioned in Chapter 4) adopted guidelines for local interchurch action, another name for ecumenical mission. The guidelines are designed to show how local churches of the nine denominations can work together. A preamble was approved which said in part that changes that will come about as the result of church union "will be worthwhile only if the church that emerges on the local level is freed to reach new levels of awareness of the liberating power of the Gospel and of the impetus which that power gives to the mission of the people of God." It also says that "local interchurch action makes provision by means of shared resources for the most effective deployment possible of laity in carrying out the full work of the church either in task forces, or through their participation in secular agencies, groups, and organizations in the humanization of our society and the world."

Local interchurch cooperation suggested in the guidelines includes:

> *Joint programs* in which two or more congregations or other local denominational units plan and operate any portion of their ministry or program jointly. Programs might include Christian education, ministries to students, pastoral counseling centers, chaplaincies to local institutions and day

care centers, job training and referral agencies and other specialized programs meeting local community needs.

Joint staff in which two or more congregations join together in employing program specialists in counseling, education, music leadership, or community service.

Joint use of building facilities in which congregations seek to eliminate costly duplication of religious facilities with their limited special uses, and to promote commonly held space for flexible uses at central location.

Cooperative or larger parishes which link congregations for common programs and ministerial leadership, usually under the direction of a parish council.

United ministry or cooperative ministry during which the congregations retain minimal ties with their denominations.[2]

In a document entitled "Structural Options for Interchurch Action in Mission Strategy," a United Presbyterian committee outlined recommendations for various options at the judicatory level and at the congregational level. Their basic philosophy was summed up as follows:

It seems clear that being "in unity for mission" is now seen by many responsible Christians as an imperative. As we are witnessing tremendous changes in the social order, and the resulting deterioration of earlier assumptions of highly individualistic solutions, we are being forced to re-think our whole concept of mission and strategy. Today's high rate of mobility, and the resulting decline of "denominational allegiances," the implications of poverty and prejudice with

[2] The guidelines for Local Interchurch Action also include the federated church, cooperative new church development, etc. Models are mentioned for each, although specific names and places are not provided.

the resulting polarization of power groups, and the overwhelming problems of the turbulently changing metropolitan centers defy any further attempts to go it alone competitively. Responsible church leaders everywhere know that to manifest visible unity requires genuine commitment to mission without which such unity is irrelevant.[3]

In *The Grass Roots Church*, Stephen Rose unfolds a plan for a cooperative ministry of clustered churches centered around specialization of function.[4] His presuppositions are essentially the same as ours: (1) that significant renewal can occur within a reformulation of the existing structures, and (2) that there are definite possibilities in the suburban situation for the church. According to his plan of restructuring, congregations in a given parish area would become specialized missional centers and ministers would be responsible for one main function. To paraphrase, Minister A would become the preacher to all the congregations in the venture. One church building would be chosen as the "chaplaincy" site or worship center. Minister B would serve as the parish pastor and counselor in another location allocated for administration of the cooperative and for pastoral counseling. Ministers C, D, and E would have charge of the teaching ministries. All ministries would be offered in the name of the cooperative ministry. It is Rose's contention that the cooperative plan allows functional specialization among clergyman, differentiation of structure, broadening of the meaning of church membership, and the combined use of congregational resources.

[3] Prepared by the special committee of the General Assembly on Interchurch Action in Presbytery and Parish, United Presbyterian Church in the U. S. A., 1968.
[4] Chap. 5.

There is no question that Rose's plan is theologically sound. From the standpoint of functional use of talents, energy, and money, as well as wise management or organizational structures, the design is certainly sociologically desirable. Unfortunately, it may prove to be psychologically naïve, especially in the suburban setting. In a few suburban locales where there may be an unusually close link among ministers or where financial doom is an obvious threat, some actualization in this direction is probably occurring. But we doubt if grass root suburbanites or grass root pastors or denominational leaders are going to accept the Rose plan in significant numbers.

The roots of division and denominationalism are probably too deep in most places for those who have been most closely involved in their establishment to do an about-face. How many ministers are going to turn over the preaching responsibility to another minister on a permanent basis? Or the counseling tasks? How many laymen in the suburban congregation which you know would buy this approach? We can argue all day that they should be willing to do so for the sake of mission, but from the standpoint of experience on the local level, our conviction is that very few pastors, much less their congregations, will be willing to move in this direction. The Rose plan may be a probable future plan for congregations not yet begun, but our opinion is that it will not be used by many existing clusters of suburban congregations.

The parish implementation of mission to the wider community in some of the approaches suggested in this chapter seem more likely to be actualized. Of course, these portray some of the features of Rose's vision, or at least similar ones. No longer is it particularly unusual to hear reports of cooperative ministries or ecumenical coalitions which incorporate shared staffs and programs and joint parish planning and action. No longer is it so unusual for suburban congregations to sponsor joint ventures involving a single parents' group, senior adult center, religious drama, a shopping center ministry, and the like.

Another option, of course, is the elimination or reduction of denominationalism itself. Sometimes two separated parties need a third reality around which they can unite, change, and gain a new perspective. Wounds may be too deep for a settlement without third-party involvement. They both might be willing to become a part of something more comprehensive than either, in which both can contribute to the new whole, and thus be related in a new and creative way.

COCU can conceivably offer a possibility along these lines in which grass roots animosities and indifference and resistance to change can be overcome by a new church. The central question about COCU, as far as we are concerned, is whether or not the plan of union will increase or decrease the missional potential of those involved. It is true that the world sees through the church's internal discrepancies. But the healing of internal divisions will mean little more than an academic achievement within the body of Christ unless the body united truly bends and expends itself in behalf of all men. There is an increasing conviction for many churchmen that mission must not be sacrificed on the altar of unity. While we argue over Mariology and the sacraments, the world is in revolution for bread and dignity.

Suprasuburban Structures Involving Missional Ecumenism

So far almost all that we have said about suburban ecumenism has presupposed an initiative directed from the local congregations. During the past several years, however, a new kind of ecumenical creature has been coming into being in a number of large metropolitan areas, such as New York, Los Angeles, and Chicago. A sampling of names for these groups includes Joint Action in Mission, Metropolitan Affairs Commission, Board for Urban Ministry, and Department of Urban Ministry. Almost without exception, these new structures operate with the following three assumptions:

1. Effective mission to secular metropolitan structures and issues means a more comprehensive planner and prophet than the local congregation. The issues are simply too huge and complex to even be envisioned, much less pragmatically penetrated, by single suburban units. Population experts tell us that the world's population will increase from its present 3.3 billion to 7 billion in the year 2000. Constantinos Doxiadis, a Greek who is one of today's foremost city planners, says that in urban terms this means that most of our cities will be at least five times as large as the cities of today. Can we begin to imagine the scale on which we will have to plan our strategy for the future?

2. The ecumenical approach for issues of race, poverty, housing, and education is the only approach. These elephantine issues defy denominational solutions and demand the maximum utilization of our resources.

3. The capacity and willingness to act is the quintessence of the cooperative structure. Visible unity is not the primary goal, but rather a potential bonus. This third assumption in particular distinguishes some of these task-oriented metropolitan groups from conventional councils of churches. The true interest is in allies for the task, not an all-inclusive ecumenical representation. When some churchmen are heard to say that they are having to decide between mission and ecumenism for

unity's sake, they are pointing to this third assumption as the crux of the matter.

As a rule, these missional ecumenical groups are made up of denominational personnel rather than representatives of local congregations. Each group reports to the denominations, not to the congregations, and presumes that the denominational unit is responsible for representing its congregations and for seeing that they implement strategy decisions. Generally speaking, these suprasuburban structures work on topical areas such as housing, poverty, education, race, and geographical area projects.[5]

In the largest cities the ecumenical mission groups are separate from the council of churches, which is likely to be geared more for inclusiveness in the interest of unity than for the missional thrusts which characterize their colleagues in the mission groups. In other cases, such as Cleveland and Rochester, the council has restructured so as to become the ecumenical mission group.

We will not take on the task of detailing the work and progress of these "beyond the local church" structures, although they do affect ecumenical work in suburbia. Our main intention in including them briefly in this chapter is to predict that in the light of ongoing urban and suburban complexity, the work of these relatively new structures will be increasingly important for the church in the 70's.

---

[5] Goodman, "New Forms for Ecumenical Cooperation for Mission in Metropolitan Areas."

8
life-giving crises

The future of the church is a future of crises. This kind of statement hardly disturbs anyone with a historical view, of course, for he knows that the past has never lacked in problems and dilemmas. Crises come at us in different ways, however, and most members of today's churches are beginning to sense that present events and those ahead are different in kind from the ones we have faced in years past. But different or the same, they are very real and very baffling. How we respond to them will determine our future.

Our use of the word "crisis" in this chapter is similar to the way in which it is used by Erik H. Erikson in *Identity, Youth, and Crisis*. He says, "It may be a good thing that the word 'crisis' no longer connotes impending catastrophe, which at one time seemed to be an obstacle to the understanding of the term. It is now being accepted as designating a necessary turning point, a crucial moment, when development must move one way or another, marshaling resources of growth, recovery, and further differentiation." [1]

The most obvious crisis concerns the survival of the institutional church. Believing that the church will exist until the end of time, we are, as stated, using Erikson's definition of crisis. The institutional church as we think of it may certainly go, but this is an "impending catastrophe" only if we have failed to understand the deeper meaning of the church.

Active participants in present-day congregations have seldom previously questioned the continued growth and prosperity of the church. But today's signs are all too obvious for intelligent Christians to deceive themselves. Proclamations about the church's decline in the measurable ways are not only unquestioned, but at times even trite. Still a greater crisis to many, however, is the loss of influence of the church indicated by public polls and apparent to any sensitive observer.

Robert Adolfs has said:

> The impression that Christianity gives is that it is becoming increasingly superfluous. And the result of this is that the Christian faith has almost been reduced to the level of a private opinion—an opinion which must be freely tolerated, but which cannot have, and cannot be allowed to have, any influence on the really important developments within our present society. This is undeniably a fact. The Christian faith plays hardly any part today, perhaps no part at all, in the really dynamic spheres of central importance in modern

[1] Erikson, *Identity, Youth, and Crisis* (New York: W. W. Norton and Co., 1968), p. 16.

society—in science, politics, economics, business life, trade, technology and the social services. What is more, the Church is unprepared, clumsy and impotent in the face of such phenomena as urbanization, automation, the population explosion and the denationalization tendencies in politics and economics. These phenomena are now ineradicably with us and are pointing to a future of further rapid change.

The Church is no longer relevant to these or other developments that are taking place within society.[2]

Other crises have pushed their way in on the church. We have already pointed to racial tensions and our participation in war. The generation gap and self-determination questions which challenge authority are not just more of the same old problems of the past. Certainly churches have grappled with a number of these concerns, and many other concerns, but not in the way that they are with us in the present. Secularization, cybernation, organ transplants, and drug usage are issues which have been thrust on us. They demand response.

Congregations have had disagreements about the way in which one should treat our "colored brethren." But who can compare these basically verbal differences of the past with the overt and consuming racial confrontations of the world in which we now live? Gone are the days of bickering about how far the Negro should be allowed to enter into society. Even in the South many white churches are beyond the arguments of integration. First of all, fewer blacks are interested in joining what they consider to be quite sterile and irrelevant congregations. The real crises come now in fear of violence, destruction, and takeover. Some of the more disturbed whites look

[2] Adolfs, *The Grave of God*, trans. by N. D. Smith (New York: Harper & Row, 1967), p. 8.

176

back longingly on those days when integration was their primary worry.

Although sounds of pacifism were heard in the church in World War I and in World War II, every historian knows that military service, our involvement in war, and our total foreign policy were never the disturbing, disruptive, and time-consuming problems in the churches that they are now. And this is no isolated crisis; it is nationwide. Furthermore, the many expressions of pacifism are only a portion of the battle cry and ferment in peace movements and individual protests which deal with seemingly endless complexities of our nation's direction. Like the racial tensions, the war questions are actually thrust directly into the church's life, and it does not have the luxury of deciding whether or not it will deal with them.

The Catholic Church is leading the way, but all churches are finding their lives shaken by the demand for self-determination on the part of a greater number of people. The under-the-table and implied authority of Protestant hierarchy is harder to get at than the more obvious strictures of the overt authoritarian bodies, but it is beginning to be pushed to the surface. Laymen are less content to hire someone to be the church for them and to pretend that they really believe in this protective procedure which serves to deceive clergy and laity. Pastors are beginning to call for a stronger voice in the beyond-the-local-church areas. This brings strain on the local parishes.

Along with the generation differences of every age have come some new problems for us. The constant friction between the young and old has new and deeper dimensions. The rapid changing of the population ratio has caused a part of the new look. The church is now set in a world that is populated mostly by young persons, and the value systems of the past are less evident. New understandings of values and meaning are struggling to be heard, and are being heard. We find ourselves responding to different surroundings than we have ever known.

The matter of music points this up. A generation ago youth could attend a high school dance on Friday evening and hear the same music that the adults would be hearing at their dance the next evening. Not so today. Much of the same music of the early 40's is still being played for adults today, but youth will have little or no part of it. Today's music is not only different in terms of volume and instruments used, but also a significant portion is far more serious, insightful, and socially sensitive than those predominantly sentimental lyrics we used to hear crooned. This change faces the church both inside and outside its walls, of course.

The process of secularization has been defined in many ways, cursed, and welcomed by churchmen. We have said something about this previously, and are using the word in the way in which Friedrich Gogarten is said to understand it, as "man's emergence from subservience under cosmic forces into a relationship of responsibility for the world." [3]

The process of secularization has come and is coming much faster than most could have guessed. It is making much church language less meaningful or perhaps exposing its meaninglessness that could be covered in the past. Liturgy has also come under fire in a more intense way than any of us has known. People are not required by their clients, customers, or employers to be good church members in this secularized age,

[3] Larry Shiner, *The Secularization of History* (Nashville: Abingdon Press, 1966), p. 26.

and they simply will not put up with the kind of dry, perfunctory words and acts that they used to endure.

Without detailing the effect of cybernation, medical research that has raised all kinds of new ethical questions about prolonging life, etc., and the impact of drug usage which has burst in on us, we should have established the fact of crises which the world has handed to the church. These are not internal crises. These are the gifts of society to which the church has been forced to relate.

How we respond to crises becomes a more relevant question than we have ever known it to be. The church has worked hard to keep life tranquil and prevent rocking the boat. Officials of the church have, without embarrassment, pointed to the pastor who has not run into trouble with his people as the man to be emulated. Tension and disagreement in a congregation have been viewed as symptoms of an unsuccessful ministry. Less than genius is required to know that the "successful" pastor is the one who keeps harmony among the membership, while continuing to glow and grow.

What a strange situation. Here we are, the body of Christ. Even the most casual glance at the event of Christ reveals tensions and conflict at every turn. We highlight a cross which is the concentration of division, suffering, and even death. Yet we routinely regard any present manifestation of such occurrences as the mark of the church's failure.

The frequent moving of pastors has enabled Methodism to avoid many of the explosions that were rapidly approaching. When pastors know that they will be moving every two or three years, they can put up with many of the potential confrontations. Laymen can endure a pastor if they can assure themselves that his days are numbered and relief will come with a new appointment. Too often we have overlooked the value of a ministry in which pastor and laymen decide that they have each other on their hands and begin to see what the relationship is really about, to find what it means to be able to struggle together in their differences.

Our churches are beginning to find very significant disagreements within the membership that can be expressed once we rid ourselves of the idea that everyone must be of one mind to be brothers. Many have assumed that failure to agree is death to a community. Therefore the pretense at agreement is widespread. Division is prolonged by attributing opposite views to a problem of semantics, or "I think that we are really getting at the same thing," or "we all have the same goals." We don't all have the same goals; differences are often far more than word differences, and we had better recognize them as such. How can we call a group of people the Church of Jesus Christ if they are unwilling to be honest with one another in their thoughts and feelings?

Robert Raines has said, "If we do have unanimity in the congregation, then it isn't the Gospel that's being preached or the real world that's being lived in." [4] Most of us will readily acknowledge this as a general truth, but when the specific disagreements and conflicts arise the generalities provide little comfort. The temptation is to try to smooth the waters at whatever cost, and the cost can very well be the life of the church.

The outward tensions of our world are making the pretense at agreement more difficult each day. People are having to state themselves. What a tremendous day for the church! The crises are calling for the kind of soul-searching that was missing in our more prosperous days. Each time the changing

[4] Quoted in Grace Ann Goodman, *Rocking the Ark*, p. 6.

world thrusts another question on us, we have another occasion to find out just what our faith is really about.

A common saying at the time of a very trying difficulty or aggravation with persons or situations is, "It is enough to make a person lose his religion." More accurately we might say, "It is enough to expose a man's *true* religion."

A theological professor and close friend of ours laments the omission of "descended into hell" from the United Methodist version of the Apostles' Creed. He maintains that such phrases force us to deal with still another aspect of life. His theme is that the church should receive gladly anything that "widens the encounter points" of life. The "hell" phrase gives us just one more question about life with which the church can work.

It is not for us to intentionally create crises and tensions within our church. Those could be phony and destructive. We work to prevent breaks and we attempt to promote understanding and increased rapport. Jesus asked that the cup be taken from him. Who is it that asks for the cross? But with Jesus the church must say, "Nevertheless . . ."

The biggest crisis of all for the church comes in a very simple way—deciding whether or not it will trust the gospel. Any congregation that spends its time saying, "If we were really serious about this . . ." or, "What we really *ought* to be doing . . . "is not the body of Christ. Franklin Littell once wrote that "no position should be verbalized until a Christian is prepared to make it a matter of disciplined witness. The business of the Church is not uttering new ideas and interpretations: it is bearing witness to the Lord of the Church and his will for men." [5]

[5] Littell, *The German Phoenix* (Garden City, N. Y.: Doubleday & Co., 1960), p. 113.

This major and primary crisis comes in the willingness of the church to listen to the world, to actually hear what is being said, to receive the world that really is and not the one it would like to pretend exists. It must then live its life in that actual world in the style that is set forth through the event of Christ. To hide from the many crises that have been previously mentioned is to deny that the word is actually the word of life in all things. It is to see grace as possible only in the kind of world which we *want* to exist.

As finite persons and creatures who see and hear in part, we have serious differences on what it means for a church to adopt the life style of Christ. We can never agree completely. Some of the problems, of course, come in our attempt to define the Christian faith by a conglomeration of remembered teachings of public school teachers, Sunday school, pastors, parents, neighborhood conversations, and various bits of logic and feelings as to the way we think Christianity ought to be. But even when we relate seriously to the community and discipline ourselves in the study and discussions that enable us to compare our understandings with what the church historically and scripturally has understood, there are still differences.

These disagreements can be most beneficial in providing the churning of the mind that is essential to every human being. We receive the opportunity of discovering again what it is to live in a community which we did not create but which has been given us. Dietrich Bonhoeffer has reminded us that the Christian is not related directly to the other Christian but related to him through God. Therefore the community they have is one that is *given* through both being related to God. Since the two did not create the bond, neither can they break it.

What will the church do when men refuse to stay in the same church with one another? Is the church wise to continue to follow directions which bring increasing numbers of people into disagreement both inside and outside the congregation and which result in members joining other churches? Certainly any sensitive group of Christians would realize that their life is called into question if fellow members choose to move, just as the group should question what kind of commitment it has if there is always peace and harmony in its midst.

But let's look again at the event of Christ. Let's look at the witness throughout the New Testament. We find no basis for shaping a church on the foundation of a lowest common denominator of belief. In our fractured understandings we are called to structure our churches as the body of Christ. This is a continual process, of course, for the expression of the faith must always be changing in order that it represent our understanding of the eternal word. But we are called to live it through, whether we prosper and grow in numbers or whether that which we have defined as the church fades from the scene.

There is suffering in this understanding, but our father in the faith, Martin Luther, has recalled to us that where there is no suffering we need not expect to find the church. And as a contemporary has said, "The church is never neat." Not if it is the Church of Jesus Christ can it be neat, for life is not neat, and the business of the church is with life.

The deceptive and finally demonic belief that people should not be offended to the degree that they leave the church is a self-defeating belief. What importance is it that a church stay in existence if it does so at the loss of its own soul? How many communities have intentionally betrayed the truth in order to retain a hundred or so members (deepening in them their own deception) while ignoring the thousands who observe this and reply with their lives if not their lips, "That kind of phony life is not for me."

We must remember that the churches which are urgently concerned to bridge the gap between what is proclaimed and what is actually lived out as a community are still in the minority. Those who choose not to relate to this kind of commitment are usually living in an urbanized society where churches are available who do not share this kind of commitment. We can hardly be accused of denying the ministry of the church to persons whom we strive to retain, but who choose to leave and who are convinced that their new church relationships are far more meaningful.

We must bear a great amount of responsibility for having deceived many of these persons into the church. If we have attracted them through well-designed and aesthetically pleasing buildings, then we have lied to them by indicating that our real interest and mission reside in the physical structures. Never mind that we plan to bring them into the "center" of the church later after this lure of the building. The trickery had already taken place. In fact, we are deceiving ourselves as well as them.

Similar deception has come through enlisting persons into many of the auxiliaries of the church—women's or men's groups, boys' and girls' baseball teams, scout organizations, and even the teaching corps of children's classes. We have maintained that they would move beyond these steps into full participation, but quite the opposite has occurred. Crises have come as these tangential members have set up forts at their points of entrance and leveled their guns at the heart of the church.

Even these crises which we unintentionally have helped create can provide life to the church. They call for deeper understandings, greater patience, and clearer insights in order to work compassionately and honestly with the persons involved. Through them we must die to any kind of self-righteousness or superiority. As creatures, we know that we are not absolute. We are called to live as those who are willing to risk our lives in the faith that the gospel we name is the means of life.

How common it is for us to believe at times that we will soon have a leveling-off place. Our churches will have faced the race issue honestly and dealt with the problems of our day in such a way that we can move back from the firing line for a while. But we know this is not the way life is. To say that we will always be facing crises is to say that life never finally levels off. Regardless of how well we have faced up to today's questions, tomorrow will bring new offenses and new temptations to lean back from the heat.

If our community is deeper than that which is based on congeniality and "getting along well with one another," then we will not be undone when we find that the obvious unity on past issues can suddenly be gone in some new crisis thrust upon us. There is sometimes a feeling of betrayal on the part of pastors or other leaders when they must take issue with those with whom they had linked arms in previous battles. But we truly betray ourselves, others, and God if our concern with one another is limited to that of remaining "friends."

We don't know the shape of tomorrow. We don't need to know the shape of tomorrow. It will bring tensions; we know that. But the faith to which we witness and on which we lay down our lives proclaims that the One who has been present bringing victory and life in the cross will be present bringing victory and life in each future moment for those who will receive this gift. We have no need to worry about whether or not the institutional church as we know it will survive. Our concern is that we give ourselves to the task of shaping it as the witness to the redemption which God is now working in this world. We can leave its future in God's hands.

The local church concerned about preserving its life will most certainly lose it, and the church that is willing to give up its life will indeed find it. This will be true whether our institutions survive or not. Rather than point us toward a fatalistic, apathetic existence, this New Testament proclamation of the word enables us to throw our whole lives into our work as those who are set free to minister. Our calling is to be faithful witnesses in a world which we claim can be received and trusted.

appendix
missional agenda:
an illustration

The opening paragraph of this book raised images of racism, war, and poverty. Each of these problems can be viewed in a wider spectrum. Poverty can be seen in relation to overpopulation and the wider welfare and income question. Racism may be seen in the wider context of national and international justice, and war can be viewed in the context of world order and international relationships. In whatever way we line these up for analysis and shake them out for discussion, we are dealing with a sizable chunk of the contextual agenda of the church's missional design for social engagement.

These issues cannot rightfully long be ignored in any sphere of the mission, whether preaching, teaching, or reaching out into the community through social action. Not only is the integrity of the church at stake, but, much more important, the future of the world is at stake in these issues. Because the church's missional design may be functionally streamlined, yet distorted in content, we have chosen to offer this Appendix to illustrate what we believe to be a top priority item on the church's missional agenda.

This item may be stated as follows in its particular contemporary historicity: The church must faithfully examine the undergirding presuppositions behind our Vietnam policies, the injustices we are perpetrating on our youth through the Selective Service system, and above all, the expanding power and influence of our military system. From a biblical perspective the item may be articulated thus: the church must be viewed as a peacemaking prophet and a voice calling for humane priorities.

The statements in this Appendix are not absolutist assertions so much as they are a passionate poking and prodding of Christian conscience on an oft-neglected item of deepest concern to the church and the world. In our intent to question radically, however, we offer what we believe is preliminary evidence for a point of view, keeping in mind that we are offering an outline of illustrative material, not a systematic treatise. In relegating this material to an Appendix, we are indicating our awareness that at certain points we are skimming the surface of some highly complex ethical problems.

The Great Offense

In our experience, there are few subjects more offensive to most suburban churchmen than the biblical emphasis on God's servant as peacemaker and reconciler among nations. Although the theme of peace is one of the magnificent obsessions of the New Testament, it has seldom been on the top shelf of the church's agenda. If there is any function that should be the church's "thing," abhorrence of war and commitment to peace would fit that description.

Missional Agenda: An Illustration

Without taking an absolute position, a Methodist minister who rejected his 4-D classification expressed it this way: "Whenever I ask somebody if they are against war, they say, 'Yes, but. . .' and then they base all their actions on the 'but.' I am making a conscious decision to build my life on the 'yes.'"[1] That the church as a whole has characteristically failed to build on the "yes" could be the church's greatest betrayal of its own gospel.

Even congregations which might be regarded as avant-garde and at the forefront of renewal are capable of considerable resistance to a position which even calls into question the Vietnam war. During 1967-68 a sizable number of families removed themselves from Northaven United Methodist Church as a result of two sermons taking a dovelike viewpoint on the war. In all fairness, it should be said in retrospect that these sermons may have been too political in overtones (offering policy directives as distinct from calling into question the moral ethos undergirding our government's policies, as Paul Ramsey puts it). Even so, when droves of people who have been members of a congregation for years cannot bear to hear two sermons which raise questions about our nation's commitment in Vietnam, one is curious why disagreement on this particular issue is so unbearable. In a few cases, charges of sedition and softness on Communism were hurled at the pastor by those who were in haste to leave. Interestingly enough, some of these persons seemed to have less difficulty in maintaining openness in relation to the racial question.

The New Testament abounds in the images of peace. Reconciliation is not peripheral or optional, but instead is central to the word. In the birth, life, and death of Jesus one theme is everywhere present. He is the prince of peace. The messengers (angels) of good news proclaim peace and goodwill among men. In the Synoptic Gospels the dove, symbol of peace, appears at Jesus' baptism. The teachings of Jesus throb with the word of goodwill, compassion, mercy, magnanimity, forgiveness, the

---

[1] A statement by the Rev. Robert G. Olmstead, in *Together*, April, 1969, p. 27.

second mile, and even love for our enemies. His life was a declaration of nonviolence.

If we take our cues from the New Testament, making sufficient allowance for the gospel's demand for justice and order and even for sophisticated theories of power in the modern world, it is difficult to escape the conclusion that participation in war from the standpoint of Christian conscience can only be justified under the most extreme and urgent conditions.

Vietnam: In the Name of Whom?

War has a way of distorting and dehumanizing the thinking of those who wage it and those who support it. Is it not bizarre that while we rightfully use words like "atrocity" and "monstrosity" to describe the Communist cruelties of killing peasants and village chiefs, we rationalize as "the inevitabilities of war" our own search-and-seize operations which kill hundreds of innocent civilians along with some Viet Cong, our use of napalm and fragmentation bombs, our tactic of crop defoliation, the torture of prisoners, and our damaging or destroying of schools, churches, pagodas, and hospitals in North Vietnam?

In the name of democracy we have been fighting a war which has uprooted over a million people from their homes. In the name of freedom and the right to vote civilians have sometimes been killed in ratios of five noncombatants for each combatant, according to newspaper reports. In the name of self-determination we have escalated a war in which by 1967 there were over 30,000 civilian amputees in South Vietnam awaiting artificial limbs. In the name of protection and pacification we have unleashed what is probably the most awesome firepower ever directed on a small, agrarian, impoverished nation, put the torch to villages, and destroyed peasant property.[2]

[2] Figures and related statements in this section are based on extensive reading over a period of many months in *The Christian Century, Christianity and Crisis, Christian Advocate, Saturday Review, The Atlantic,* and other journals.

For ourselves and our own land some Americans may say "better dead than red," but what business do we have supporting this doctrine in someone else's land where those destroyed have frequently been the people we are "saving" from Communism? By what diabolical, perverted logic do we make decisions to destroy a village "in order to save it"?[3] To survey the extent of the annihilation, the suffering, and the terror caused by the war in Vietnam is of necessity to raise the question, "Could anything be worse than this?"

While we have been destroying people and property with massive violence in Vietnam, our own land has been threatened economically, psychologically, and morally by our Vietnam policy. While our cities decay and the cauldron of our cultural milieu boils to dangerous levels, we have been spending $2 billion monthly in a controversial cause across the world. While we have sought to pacify villages whose names we cannot pronounce, we are barely able to pacify our own riot-torn metropolises and campuses.

In a time when we are in desperate need of cultivating all possible resources of compassion and reconciliation within our own land, the psychology of violence infiltrates the foundations of our thinking and communicating, making us a people whose ears are attuned to bombing reports, United States casualty lists, and body counts of how many Cong have been "bagged." At a time when we have been in dire need of confidence in our national leaders, the nation's youth are beset by an increasing erosion of confidence in the national destiny.

One does not have to look to the New Testament to ask whether or not we have embarked on a self-defeating course. The contradiction of trying to be world policeman and becoming increasingly impotent to manage our own household should be persuasive evidence that our course of action is self-destructive in the most pragmatic sense.

[3] Associated Press article by Peter Arnett concerning Ben Tre, Vietnam, in the *Dallas Morning News,* February 8, 1968.

Christ's Suburban Body

The authors are well aware of sophisticated arguments by some American theologians, philosophers, and statesmen seeking to justify United States presence in Vietnam, if not all of our actions. Of course, there are equally recognized moral theologians and public figures who take the opposite point of view, that is, consistent in direction with the position here taken. Whatever position an individual has adopted or chooses to adopt in the future, the church *as church* must at least confront us with questions like these: (1) Does the church have anything to say about Vietnam which differs from the standards of our society? (2) Has the state become the golden calf of our age, so that people are willing to trust to it an incredible power and "rightness" which it should not have? (3) Has war become so integral to our economy that the health of the free enterprise system, to say nothing of our psychic and emotional resources, is now dependent on a war system?

The Growing Complex

The ominous specter of a growing military-industrial complex is a question which the church ignores only at great peril for both church and state. General David Shoup, former Commandant of the United States Marine Corps, warned of the new American militarism in an article by that name in *The Atlantic Monthly* of April, 1699. He asserts that "America has become a militaristic and aggressive nation" since World War II, fueled by the burgeoning military establishment and associated industries.

Somewhat like a religion, the basic appeals of anti-Communism, national defense, and patriotism provide the foundation for a powerful creed upon which the defense establishment can build, grow, and justify its cost. More so than many large bureaucratic organizations, the defense establishment now devotes a large share of its efforts to self-perpetuation, to justifying its organizations, to preaching its doctrines, and to self-maintenance and management.

Missional Agenda: An Illustration

Warfare becomes an extension of war games and field tests. War justifies the existence of the establishment, provides experience for the military novice and challenges for the senior officer. Wars and emergencies put the military and their leaders on the front pages and give status and prestige to the professionals. Wars add to the military traditions, the self-nourishment of heroic deeds, and provide a new crop of military leaders who become the rededicated disciples of the code of service and military action. Being recognized public figures in a nation always seeking folk heroes, the military leaders have been largely exempt from the criticism experienced by the more plebian politician. Flag officers are considered "experts," and their views are often accepted by press and Congress as the gospel. In turn, the distinguished military leader feels obliged not only to perpetuate loyally the doctrine of his service but to comply with the stereotyped military characteristics by being tough, aggressive, and firm in his resistance to Communist aggression and his belief in the military solutions to world problems. Standing closely behind these leaders, encouraging and prompting them, are the rich and powerful defense industries. Standing in front, adorned with service caps, ribbons, and lapel emblems, is a nation of veterans—patriotic, belligerent, romantic, and well intentioned, finding a certain sublimation and excitement in their country's latest military venture. Militarism in America is in full bloom and promises a future of vigourous self-pollination—unless the blight of Vietnam reveals that militarism is more a poisonous weed than a glorious blossom.[4]

Senator Eugene McCarthy has called the military-industrial-academic establishment "a republic within the Republic." Writing in the December 21, 1968, *Saturday Review*, McCarthy said of the Defense Department, "With military missions in many nations of the world, with its own intelligence operations . . . , with its own business of selling billions of dollars worth of arms—for cash or on credit—all around the world, with its involvement now in 'civic action' or 'nation-building' in many of the underdeveloped countries, the Defense Department has become perhaps the strongest independent power in world affairs." [5] In McCarthy's judgment, Defense Department actions are to a large extent beyond the effective control of Congress because of its influence on foreign, domestic, and educational policies.

It seems indisputable that the American economy is increasingly tied to military-related expenditures. Figures from the Friends Committee on National Legislation have indicated that 66 percent of funds voted by Congress in 1968 were for military and defense-related items.[6] The nonmilitary balance of 34 percent allowed 15 percent for health, education, and welfare. In dollar amounts for 1968, the picture looked like this:

Military Activities	81 billion
Veterans and Other Costs of Past Wars	7 billion
Administration of National Debt (More than 75% War Created)	15 billion
Economic Aid to the Developing World	2 billion
Human Needs at Home (Welfare, Housing, Education, Health)	24 billion

When we consider what conceivably could be done with some of the funds now being allocated for military technology and hardware ($77 billion in 1970 for the Department of Defense), what does it mean if we continue the priorities now in force? In 1969 a medium bomber costs $7 million. The latest nuclear attack

[5] McCarthy, "The Pursuit of Military Security," *Saturday Review,* December 21, 1968.
[6] Friends Committee on National Legislation, Washington Newsletter, No. 299, December, 1968.

submarine has a price tag of $77 million. Aircraft carriers are being built for $277 million.[7] Most defense industries have publicly stated that they look forward to a post-Vietnam world filled with military and space business. Ever expanding arms budgets are expected to continue as a "defense" oriented business based on sophisticated new weaponry and new rounds in the arms race. Where will this spiraling spending eventually lead us?

An instrument of what seems to us to be an increasing war mentality is the Selective Service system, which has been operative since 1940. Many youth see it as a representation of the adult world, the adult system, the way adults deal with youth. Our youth have experienced a system that requires them to register at eighteen, subjects them to the possibility of being drafted by the time they are nineteen. These same youth are not allowed the privilege of ballot power. They have no legal rights as adults, yet they are judged by the system to be adult enough to serve in the armed forces, to be trained to kill if necessary, to risk being killed, and to make decisions affecting the lives of other men. What does it communicate to youth about the adult system when they are given no political voice through ballot power to influence the system which consigns them to military service?

Many adults in this nation have forgotten that military conscription on an ongoing basis has been alien to the American way of life. In spite of that fact, the present Selective Service System has been in effect since 1940, except for a seventeen-month interlude in 1947-48. Many adults have come to take the draft for granted, as though it represented American tradition and ideals. Many of our forefathers came to the United States in order to escape compulsory military conscription in European nations. They were not thought of as draft evaders by their new countrymen. Today thousands of American youth have migrated to Canada or other countries for similar reasons. Surely this should cause us grave concern about our nation's draft system.

[7] *Ibid.*

In addition to the fact that the draft has become a part of our way of life, there are many inequities in the system itself. There are practically no qualifications for draft board membership, except residence and the requirement that one must retire from the board at the age of seventy-five. In most cases there is no training in either the intricacies of the draft system or in theological positions related to the just war theory and conscientious objection. This means that we have turned over the most valuable asset in our nation—the youth—to boards composed of people who have virtually no qualifications to judge requests for conscientious objection intelligently and fairly. Some draft board members do not even know the various deferments allowable within the system. In many areas of the country where there is a heavy percentage of black people, there has never been a black member of the draft board. Is this lack of proportionate racial representation the kind of justice that adults wish to hold before our youth?

There are very few uniform Selective Service system standards throughout the country. Conscientious objectors appearing before one board may be granted the CO status, but would be rejected by another board on the very same set of requests. The destiny of many young men in this nation has been placed in the hands of those whose very job is to deliver a certain quota of draftees monthly to induction centers. Can this system with its vested interest in "delivery" be expected to maintain open minds and nonprejudicial hearings? In addition, a retired army general has been the head of this alleged civilian agency for almost thirty years. Does this system, with its obviously stacked deck, represent the kind of justice that we want to communicate to our youth?

Many youth have pointed out that the deferment system is based on educational advantage, which is essentially deferment by social and economic class. This method indirectly fosters an elitist system by selecting those who follow the prescribed courses in higher education or selected occupations "in the national interest." The poor and the minority groups are discriminated against once again, since they do not, as a rule, have the educational advantages. Those who receive the least benefits in our society are regarded by the system as the most expendable. It doesn't take too much imagination to realize that those who set up the deferment system are not very interested in jobs that might change the status quo. There are no deferments for youth who want to work in civil rights or for those who want to write poetry or for those who have the opportunity to teach in certain schools. These are apparently not regarded as being "in the national interest."

Whereas the draft laws allow only a legally acceptable choice between objection to all wars or objection to none, the religious heritage of many youth in our nation has been based on the just war theory. This theory by its nature means that some wars have been regarded by Christians as the better of two evils, while other wars have been thought to be intolerable or not within a just war tradition. This implies the need for selective objection, that is, for some kind of responsible judgment as to whether or not a war can be fought in good conscience.

Hundreds of youth of our nation are having to assume a new personal and social role, namely that of criminal, in order to be faithful to their religious convictions. That which is regarded by the state as civil disobedience is regarded by some youth as religious obedience. The National Council of Churches, the National Conference of Roman Catholic Bishops, the American Baptist Convention, the Disciples of Christ, the United Church of Christ, the Reformed Church in America, and the Lutheran Church in America have all endorsed the concept of selective objection without punishment from the state. In September, 1969, the bishops of the Episcopal Church requested political amnesty for draft resisters.

Churchmen should be courageous enough to make it clear that they will offer support both to those youths who choose to participate in the Selective Service system and to those who in one way or another are conscientious or selective objectors. It has been a sad spectacle in this nation when so few churchmen, both clergy and laity, have been willing to offer even moral support to those youths who, out of their religious convictions, could not in sound conscience fight the war in Vietnam.

The authors have attempted to provide a glimpse of our national life and priorities as we see them reflected in Vietnam, the growing power of the military system, and the Selective Service system. Our nation is going to have to choose between two futures. One future is military-oriented, with the United States adopting the role of a world gendarme who is a domestic cripple, increasingly dependent psychologically and economically on the war system.

The other future is based on the premise that our greatest gift to mankind resides in making the American ideal into a workable model where our example in our own cities may become an incarnate vision for mankind. If we can demonstrate a society whose people increasingly breathe the fresh air of human dignity and freedom, whose institutions are relatively humane agents of change, then in our judgment we will be fulfilling our true national destiny. If this is to happen, some present priorities are going to have to be shaken to the foundations. Where will the voice of the church be?

The hour may already be growing late in the United States for the reversability of militarism. The web of economic, political, and social vested interests is entangling a larger and larger segment of the society. However, it is heartening that the peace movement, managing some influence with and through the general public, apparently played a significant role in policy determination in the last year of the Johnson administration, and to some extent during the first year of President Nixon's term.

It is our fervent hope that at least some of the material in this Appendix will be obsolete before it reaches the public (as a politically realistic hope, a draft system with less inequities, removal of substantial numbers of American troops from Vietnam, and partial de-escalation of militarism). The announcement in September, 1969, of the 50,000 quota reduction in the November and December draft figures is at least a step in the right direction.

If there are enough public voices raised against the course of action we have been pursuing in our national priorities, creative change can be made possible. Hopefully, additional suburban churchmen will join the chorus for more imaginative and mature foreign and domestic policies.

Nothing in our critique of the position and power of the military establishment should be interpreted as an attack on the legitimate existence of a military force or on the many individuals who compose that system. Some of the most humane Americans are to be found in the professional military service. However, we do see militarism in ascendancy, and we do believe this condition can only bring misery to our nation as it has to others where national policy has been increasingly subservient to the military establishment.

The responsibility for our plight is upon all of us. In one way or another most of us have glorified war by conversation, by TV and movie consumption, or by delegating a degree of authority to military leaders that we would not even think of handing over to any other source—corporation, family, spouse, or church. But we are all implicated by commission or omission. By analogy we might say that many Christians are convinced that today's funeral practices frequently represent a departure from genuine Christian values. Whenever this is so, we as Christians have mainly ourselves to blame. Many Protestant pastors have failed to exercise the authority they do have and have usually laid more of the blame on the morticians than has been justified. The Pentagon may have something like an independent power and momentum of its own, but fundamentally it is in reality the visible brain trust for the value system of the American people.

Perspectives for Peacemaking

The Christian bag is full of implications for an expanding ideological prism. Perspectives for peacemaking arise from the Christian insistence that our "enemies" are human beings. Many

Americans have not seen the North Vietnamese people as human beings. If we had, we would not have rained down death on their cities and farmlands, on their women and children. The North Vietnamese are frequently thought of as a "homogeneous" blob, an embodiment of doctrines considered to be evil. If we can mentally herd them into a menacing ideological abstraction, they become expendable in wholesale numbers.

Senator William Fulbright remarks that "man's capacity for decent behavior seems to vary directly with his perception of others, as individual humans with human motives and feelings, whereas his capacity for barbarous behavior seems to increase with his perception of an adversary in abstract terms. This is the only explanation I can think of for the fact that the very same good and decent citizens who would never fail to feed a hungry child or comfort a sick friend . . . can celebrate the number of Viet Cong killed in a particular week or battle, talk of 'making a desert' of North Vietnam or of 'bombing it back into the Stone Age' despite the fact that most, almost all, of the victims would be innocent peasants and workers." [8]

In a similar vein, Dr. Brock Chisolm, Canadian psychiatrist and formerly head of the World Health Organization, observed that "what we the people of the world need is to exercise our imaginations, to develop our ability to look at things from outside our accidental area of being." [9] Our ideologies are acquired through the accidental area of our birth, except in rare cases. If you are born in Russia, the chances are overwhelming that you will be a part of the Communist system. If you are born in Muleshoe, Texas, the odds are outstanding that you will be a devotee of the democratic system. The church's task is to expand the capacity of suburbanites for empathetic imagination, universality of concern, and an accent on a reconciling quality to our personal and collective lives.

[8] Fulbright, *The Arrogance of Power* (New York: Vintage Books, 1966), p. 165.
[9] Quoted in *Ibid.*, p. 167.

Missional Agenda: An Illustration

Perspectives for peacemaking arise from the Christian belief that the most effective weapon of change, except in the rarest of situations, is in example to others, not elimination of others. This fact is being hammered out on the anvil of our generation, calling itself by many names—the spirit movement, the civilizing process, the human revolution. Black Power has been saying, "If you have anything to offer, then you'd best begin with your own scene."

The weapons of truth, reconciliation, and personal example require more of us than missiles, napalm, and new military bases. It is more demanding to rebuild our cities and work for a national unity than to use violence across the world. Because from a policy standpoint it is less demanding to destroy or eliminate than to create and rebuild, war is often the tool of those who are losing the capacity to re-create their own society. When the policy of international violence begins to outweigh the internal resources for self-development, we have cause for concern and lamentation. Our best long-range weapon is not a system of sophisticated military missiles, but instead an example of a working democracy.

Many of the youth understand this better than the older adult generation. Somehow the younger generation is populated with those who know the ancient Christian wisdom—you cannot eliminate a competing ideology by violence. You can only outexample it or, in today's situation, outmaneuver it with a mature international policy. As Pope John XXIII revealed in his Pacem in Terris, plenty of youth know that military "solutions" are not solutions for political, economic, and social problems.

These students should be congratulated for their aversion to the horrors of napalmed civilians, the pathology of an international violence which makes some people wealthy through the destruction of their fellowmen, and the gross inequities in our national life. They are asking the adults who control the system, "Why do we call it hoodlumism when ghetto residents loot and burn or when protesting students take over a campus, but call it military strategy when we reduce a village to rubble in order to save it? How can we live by the sword abroad and expect to live by the olive branch at home?"

By and large the suburban church has reflected the nationalistic value system of the culture instead of elevating a call to peace to place of priority on its missional agenda. The church could make a substantial contribution to the future of man by ceasing its acquiescence to the war system and becoming a militant for peace.

index

Index

Inner City, the, 18, 21, 26-27, 30-33, 69, 71
Institute for Middle Class Reformers, 30-31
Institutional narcissism, 88
Integration, 176-77
Interchurch action, 163-71
Issue Forum, The, 154

Jesus, 41, 44, 49-51, 54-55, 57, 109, 181
Jewish congregation, 112-13, 152, 155
Jewish community, 24
John Birch Society, 135, 139
Joint Action in Mission, 172
Joint staff, 168, 171
Joy, 64
Judgment, 48, 54
Judson Memorial Church, New York City, 125, 132
Justice, 41, 53-54, 71, 80, 82, 87, 135-36

Kerner Commission, 22-23
Kerygma, 60-63
Koinonia, 60, 62

Laymen, 78, 130, 140, 167, 170, 177, 179-80
Le Corbusier's Chapel, 100
Let's Work Together, 21
Letter writing, 140-41
Liberation, 41, 47-53, 68, 70, 73
gospel of, 95, 167
social, 56
Life style, 40-41, 110, 182
Littell, Franklin, 181
Living room dialogue, 146
Local Church Looks to the Future, The, 115n
Love, 47, 53, 71, 78
Lundin, Jack W., 109
Luther, Martin, 46, 183
Lutheran Church in America, 33, 107, 109

Metropolitan Affairs Commission, 172
Mexican-American, 142, 153
Midas International Foundation, 31
"Mighty Fortress Is Our God, A," 47, 147
Mill, John Stuart, 75
Mills, C. Wright, 35
Missions, Commission on, 137
Mobility, 28-29, 106, 116, 168
Montbello (Denver), Colo., 114-15
Moody, Howard, 125
motive magazine, 100, 157, 159
Music, 161, 168, 178

Nation, 18, 19, 22
National Advisory Commission on Civil Disorders, 22-23
National Conference on Church Architecture, 101
National Conference on Religious Architecture, 106
National Council of Churches, 80
New Creation as Metropolis, The, 28n
New York Times, The, 31n
Niebuhr, Richard, 60, 61
Noise of Solemn Assemblies, The, 65n, 67-68
Nominations and Personnel Committee, 126
Northaven United Methodist Church, 75-77, 112, 151, 156-58, 189
North Dallas Cooperative Ministry, the, 151-63, 165

"Of Black America," 23
Ogden, Schubert, 42n, 57n
On Not Leaving It to the Snake, 38
Outler, Albert C., 147

Parish, 71-73, 169. See also Church, local
Parish Institute, 155
Parish School of Theology, 155

Index

Pastor, 33, 140, 167, 169-70, 182
 and laity, 84, 177, 179-80
 role of, 128-31
Pastoral Psychology, 26n
Pastoral care, 91
Paternalism, 139, 142
Perkins School of Theology, 147
Pharisees, 49
Pogo, 19
Polarization, 18, 80, 133, 166, 169
Police, 22, 35, 71
Politics, 28-29, 32, 47, 70-71, 79,
 88, 98, 142, 158-59, 162, 164-
 65, 176
Poor People's Campaign, 81
Population explosion, 28, 176
Port Huron Statement, The, 161
Potential, 25-30, 64
Poverty, 23, 55, 105, 168, 172-73
Power, 21, 26, 70-72, 130
 Black, 21, 71, 201
 church, 34-36, 71
 groups, 169
 suburban, 31, 34-36
Power Elite, The, 35
Preaching, 58, 88, 170, 189
Prejudice, 168. *See also* Racism
Presbyterian Church, 33, 103, 106,
 112-15, 124, 143, 148, 151-52,
 164-65, 168, 169n
Priesthood of all believers, 83
Priorities, 18, 25, 30, 98, 105, 125,
 150, 198
Project Equality, 71, 97
Project Misdemeanant, 97
Prophets, 41, 83
Prophetic posture, 74, 83
Protestant, 145, 147-48, 155, 166
Protestantism in Suburban Life,
 26n

Quaker, 165

Race, 134, 172-73, 176-77, 185
Racism, 21, 23-24, 33, 164
Raines, Robert, 180
Reality of God, The, 42n, 57n

Reductionism, 67
Reformed Church in America, 114
"Responsibility of the Church for
 Society, The," 60-61
Riots, 21, 25
Rocking the Ark, 82, 124, 180n
Rose, Stephen C., 62, 169-70

Sacrament(s), 90, 150, 158, 171
St. Mark's Church, 114
St. Stephen United Methodist
 Church, 100-101, 103, 146-48
Schaller, Lyle, 26, 35, 72, 93n,
 115n
School(s), 21, 24, 56, 72, 139,
 161, 165, 178, 182
Schulz, Charles M., 48
Schutz, William, 64
Second Vatican Council, 144, 146-
 47
Secular, 37
 agencies, 84, 117
 books, 37
 Christianity, 40
 image, 39
 instinct, 39
 man, 19, 41-43
 organizations, 117
 mind, 38, 41
Secular City, The, 37, 42n, 61
Secular Meaning of the Gospel,
 The, 37, 42
Secularism, 42
Secularity, 39, 40, 42
 Christian, 40, 57
Secularization, 42, 176, 178
Secularization of History, The, 37,
 178
Selective Service system, 35, 195-99
Self-determination, 120-21, 139,
 176-77
Selfhood, 39, 47-51
Servanthood, 55, 64, 89, 116
Shepherding, 61, 78-79
Shiner, Larry, 178n
Shippey, Frederick, 26n
Sin, 38, 79

207